UNDERSTANDING TEXTILES
A Laboratory Manual

Phyllis G. Tortora
Eleanor Hall Nelson
Constance Gerry Sussman
Department of Home Economics
Queens College

Macmillan Publishing Co., Inc.
New York
Collier Macmillan Publishers
London

Printed in the United States of America

Macmillan Publishing Co., Inc.
866 Third Avenue, New York, New York 10022

Collier Macmillan Canada, Ltd.

ISBN 0-02-420930-9

Printing: 1 2 3 4 5 6 7 8   Year: 8 9 0 1 2 3 4

PREFACE

The purpose of this laboratory manual is to illustrate basic concepts for students who undertake the study of textiles for the first time. The manual is designed to be used with the text *Understanding Textiles*, and the sequence of development of material in this manual parallels the development of that book. Related readings from the text are cited, although instructors who are using other texts may find that with some modifications the manual could be adapted for use with the text they are using.

The major problem confronting the authors in writing this manual was the realization that one manual cannot satisfy the requirements of all introductory textiles courses. Nevertheless, it was necessary to try to meet the varying needs of different institutions that have different programs, class sizes, and resources. For this reason the manual is structured to include some activities that could be done in the classroom or at home as well as more complex activities that require a laboratory setting. It is our hope that instructors will find the material sufficiently flexible so that it can be adapted to meet the needs of students attending different types of institutions. Many institutions have had to increase class size to the point where the traditional laboratory has had to be eliminated. Those activities that students can carry out independent of the classroom or laboratory may prove helpful in such classes.

The manual is intended for use with a first course in textiles and therefore stresses the simpler types of tests that do not utilize elaborate testing equipment. For those institutions that have equipment available, technical tests are cited. It is recommended that instructors demonstrate or instruct students in the use of this equipment. Specific instructions for these tests were not included, since the publications of the AATCC and the ASTM outline them in detail. Furthermore, institutions may own different models of the same type of testing equipment, and space does not permit the inclusion of instructions for all types and models of testing equipment.

For those instructors with limited time and space, the adaptation of some of the experiments for demonstration purposes is recommended. Many of the chemical solubility tests, for example, might be handled in this way, and the imaginative instructor will undoubtedly see other such tests that lend themselves to demonstration. Some activities are noted as particularly useful for assignment as research projects for individual or groups of students. For example, the summary activity in Unit Seven, Part 2 could be adapted as a term project.

Guidelines for the use of the manual by the instructor are included in Appendix C. This section provides special notes concerning materials, sources of items that may be difficult to obtain, special considerations in selecting materials, and notes on organization of the laboratory.

Contents

	Manual Page	Related Readings in the Text, *Understanding Textiles*
UNIT ONE Textile Fibers and Their Properties	5	Chapters 1 and 2
Part 1: Generic and Trademark Fiber Names	5	Chapter 1, pp. 6–7
Part 2: Textile Fiber Products Identification Act	6	Chapter 1, pp. 7–9
Part 3: Physical Properties of Textile Fibers	7	Chapter 1, pp. 9–20
Part 4: Chemical Properties of Textile Fibers	20	Chapter 2
Part 5: Generic Textile Fibers	28	Chapters 3 to 12
UNIT TWO Yarns	37	Chapter 13
Part 1: Yarn Construction	37	Chapter 13, p. 153–170
Part 2: Determining the Direction of Yarn Twist	41	Chapter 13, p. 170–171
Part 3: Types of Yarns	43	Chapter 13, p. 171–178
Part 4: Yarn Analysis	46	Chapter 13, p. 171–178
UNIT THREE Fabric Construction	49	Chapters 14, 15, 16
Part 1: Introduction	49	Chapter 14
Part 2: Woven Fabrics	53	Chapter 14
A. Basic Weaves—The Plain Weave	53	Chapter 14, pp. 190–193
B. Basic Weaves—Plain Weave Variations	59	Chapter 14, p. 193
C. Basic Weaves—The Twill Weave	63	Chapter 14, pp. 194–195
D. Basic Weaves—The Satin Weave	67	Chapter 14, pp. 195–197
E. Fancy Weaves—Jacquard, Dobby, and Others	69	Chapter 14, pp. 197–198
F. Other Weaves	71	Chapter 14, pp. 198–216
Part 3: Knitted Fabrics	77	Chapter 15
A. Filling or Weft Knits	78	Chapter 15, pp. 222–226
B. Warp Knits	84	Chapter 15, pp. 226–229
C. Distinguishing Warp and Filling Knits	87	Chapter 15, p. 222–229
D. Performance of Knit Fabrics	89	Chapter 15, p. 229–231
Part 4: Other Fabric Constructions	95	Chapter 16
A. Nets, Lace, Macrame, and Crochet	95	Chapter 16, pp. 234–240
B. Stitch-through Fabric Construction	96	Chapter 16, pp. 240–242
C. Fabric Webs	97	Chapter 16, pp. 242–249
UNIT FOUR Dyeing and Printing	101	Chapters 17, 18
Part 1: Dyeing	101	Chapter 17, pp. 251–259
Part 2: Colorfastness	105	Chapter 17, pp. 259–260
Part 3: Printing	113	Chapter 18

	Manual Page	Related Readings in Text
UNIT FIVE Finishes	115	Chapter 19, 20
Part 1: Classification of Finishes	115	Chapter 19, pp. 288–289
Part 2: Finishes Affecting Appearance	116	Chapter 19, pp. 289–302
Part 3: Finishes Affecting Performance	119	Chapter 20
UNIT SIX Care of Fabrics and Textiles and the Environment	129	Chapters 21, 22
Part 1: Care Labeling	129	pp. 19, 20, 31
Part 2: Laundry Additives	129	Chapter 21, pp. 327–340
Part 3: Stain Removal	133	Chapter 21, pp. 337–340
Part 4: Textiles and the Environment	136	Chapter 22
UNIT SEVEN Textile Testing and Performance Evaluation	139	Chapters 23, 24
Part 1: Levels of Testing	139	Chapter 23
Part 2: Evaluation of Textile Products	145	Chapter 23, 24
Appendixes		
A. Bibliography	151	
B. Students' Appendix	155	
C. The Instructor's Guide to the Use of the Manual	159	

INTRODUCTION

This laboratory manual provides a series of activities, tests, and/or experiments that serve to illustrate basic concepts in the field of textiles. These activities require very little technical skill or previous experience in a laboratory. They do, however, require a scientific approach in the sense that preliminary organization, following of instructions, and careful observation of results and recording of data are essential if one is to achieve accurate results.

In addition to accuracy and care in following instructions, those who work in a laboratory setting should follow the safety precautions outlined by the instructor. Dangerous chemical substances are sometimes used in experiments and must be handled with care and with the appropriate equipment. Other experiments involve the use of a Bunsen burner or a lighted candle, and caution should be taken to avoid any hazards from fire. Note the location of fire extinguishers before conducting any tests using flammable materials.

In reading the material in the manual, students should note that distinctions are drawn between the laboratory activities and tests as outlined in this manual and the technical tests developed and used for research or in the textile industry. If the laboratory in which you are working is equipped with the apparatus that is used in technical testing, the instructor may demonstrate the use of this equipment or ask students to use it in some of the experiments. In some institutions a separate course in textile testing is taught and students will become more familiar with this equipment in subsequent courses. Because this manual is designed for a first course in textiles, it stresses simpler, less technical activities.

The appendixes contain instructions on the use of certain basic laboratory equipment such as the microscope and the linen tester. A brief review of these instructions before using this equipment may facilitate the completion of work requiring their use.

The following guidelines will make for better results in the laboratory work.

1. Read references in the text or assigned reference materials carefully and completely before beginning work in the laboratory.

2. Read through *all of the instructions* for an experiment before beginning the experiment.

3. Before beginning experiments, assemble all of the supplies and equipment necessary for that experiment.

4. Be sure to complete each step of the experiment before going on to the next.

5. Record data at the time of observation, not later, so that the data is accurate.

6. Mount the samples used in the experiments whenever possible. Space has been provided at the back of the manual for mounting large samples. Directions for mounting samples are included in Appendix B.

   The instructor will select from the experiments outlined in the manual those that are most appropriate for each laboratory and/or textiles course, so that not all of the activities outlined in the book will be done by each student. In some instances groups will be organized to carry out a particular part of an experiment. Instructors may recommend procedures using equipment or supplies that differ from those listed in the manual. Be sure to follow these instructions with care.

Notations

Measurements. The metric measurements included in parentheses are rounded off to the nearest correct equivalent. They are not intended to be exact.

Time. An approximation of the time required for the tests or experiments is provided throughout the manual. The code is as follows: * = less than 15 minutes, ** = less than 30 minutes, *** = less than one hour, and **** = less than two hours.

UNIT ONE

Textile Fibers and Their Properties

PART 1: GENERIC AND TRADEMARK FIBER NAMES

References Chapter 1, *Understanding Textiles*, assigned readings in texts or reference books, *A Dictionary of Textile Terms* by Dan River Mills, Inc., *Textile Glossary*, by Marvin Klapper, and *American Fabrics Encyclopedia.*[1]

(1) One of the first tasks that students face when undertaking the study of a technological field is to master the vocabulary of that field. The following are a few textile terms that should be understood before the remainder of this section can be completed. Define each of these terms.

1. textile fiber

2. natural fiber

3. man-made fiber

4. generic fiber name

5. trademark fiber name

(2) The following is a list of the contents of an imaginary fabric. Underline all of the generic fiber names in this list. Circle all of the trademarks.

     50% cotton

     20% Avril rayon

     15% Crepeset nylon

     10% silk

      5% Lycra spandex

[1]See the Bibliography in Appendix A for complete bibliographical citations on all references.

PART 2: TEXTILE FIBER PRODUCTS IDENTIFICATION ACT

References Chapter 1, *Understanding Textiles* or assigned readings in text or reference books.

The government regulates the labeling of textile products in order to provide the consumer with accurate information about these products. After reading the section in the text concerning the Textile Fiber Products Identification Act (TFPIA), students should note the requirements of and the exceptions to the Act. (1) Two facsimiles of labels are reproduced in A. and B. Examine each one, and then read the directions that follow each label.

A. 80% Dacron polyester

   20% wool

   Wash in lukewarm water, line dry

   Press with cool, not hot, iron

   ID #33345

   Made in Hong Kong

1. Circle all information on this label that is required by the TFPIA.
2. Underline all information on this label that is *not* required by the TFPIA.

B. SILKEE BLOUSE

   20% Dacron

   15% rayon

   2% silk

   remainder is cotton

   Manufactured by the Smith Co., N.Y., N.Y.

1. In what ways does this label violate the TFPIA?
2. Rewrite the label so that it conforms to the TFPIA requirements.

(2) In the space that is provided design a correct label for a bathing suit manufactured by the XYZ Company of Smithtown, N.Y., which is made of a blend of Dacron (40%), cotton (50%), Lycra (5%), and 5% of miscellaneous, unknown fiber. The trim is 100 per cent cotton.

PART 3: PHYSICAL PROPERTIES OF TEXTILE FIBERS

Each of the following laboratory activities is meant to illustrate a physical property of textile fibers. In some instances only observation will be required; in others an activity or experiment will serve to illustrate the concept. Later, when the study is focused on specific textile fibers, similar activities and/or experiments will be carried out with a number of different fibers. *The following activities are not technical tests of textile fibers.* They lack adequate control of conditions and they generate no objective standards for evaluation. The activities will, however, serve to clarify certain terms and concepts. References Chapter 1 *Understanding Textiles* or assigned readings in text or reference books.

A. Fiber Properties Relating to Appearance

*1. *Color*

Textile fibers differ in their natural color. Samples of each of four different fibers are provided for examination.

Materials and Apparatus
    One small bundle of each of these fibers:
    unbleached cotton
    wool, in the grease (unscoured)
    acetate
    nylon

Procedure

1. Observe the samples and compare them in relation to color.

2. Describe the color of each of the samples in the spaces provided.

Sample 1 unbleached cotton	Sample 2 wool (unscoured)	Sample 3 acetate	Sample 4 nylon
_____	_____	_____	_____
_____	_____	_____	_____
_____	_____	_____	_____
_____	_____	_____	_____
_____	_____	_____	_____

*2. *Microscopic Appearance*

Most single fibers are so small that they require magnification with a microscope[2] in order to examine the physical appearance of the fibers.

(1) Longitudinal appearance of fibers

Materials and Apparatus

microscope with slides of longitudinal view of wool, cotton, regular nylon, and regular viscose rayon

or

photomicrographs of longitudinal views of wool, cotton, regular nylon, and regular viscose rayon from text and/or reference materials provided by the instructor

Procedure

1. Examine the slides or photographs of the longitudinal views of the fibers.

2. Describe the appearance of the fiber.

Fiber	*Appearance*
1. wool	
2. cotton	
3. regular nylon	
4. regular viscose rayon	

(2) Striations

Striations are lengthwise lines that appear on the surface of some man-made fibers when they are viewed under the microscope. Which one of the four fibers in the photomicrographs has striations? _____

The following are some cross-sectional diagrams of fibers that possess striations and some that do not.

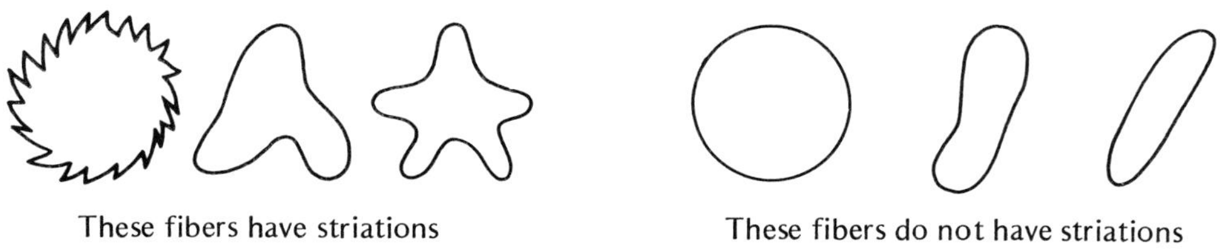

These fibers have striations   These fibers do not have striations

Diagram 1-1.

[2]See Appendix B for instructions on how to use the microscope.

From these diagrams what can be concluded about the causes of striations?

_____

_____

_____

_____

*3. *Luster*

(1) *Luster* is the sheen or light reflectance of a fiber. It is often more obvious in the yarn or fabric made from that fiber. Different fibers possess varying degrees of luster.

Materials and Apparatus
      small bundles of cotton, silk, bright acetate, and dull acetate fibers
      flat surface
      source of artificial light

Procedure

1. Place the samples side by side on a flat surface under a direct source of light. Be sure that the light shines evenly on all four samples.

2. Compare the luster of the samples on the following chart.

Chart 1-1. LUSTER OF SELECTED FIBERS		
Sample	Luster (Check Off One Rating)	
	High Luster	Medium Luster	Low Luster
Cotton			
Silk			
Bright acetate			
Dull acetate			

(2) Note that the sample of bright acetate fiber has a higher luster than the sample of dull acetate. Man-made fibers may be delustered by adding titanium dioxide to the fiber. This *delusterant* shows up in the microscopic view of the fiber. Examine either a prepared slide of a delustered fiber or a photomicrograph from the text or from a reference source.
How does the delusterant affect the microscopic appearance of the fiber?

*4. *Crimp*
      Some natural fibers possess an undulating or wavy shape known as *crimp*, whereas others do not. Man-made fibers can have crimp added during the manufacturing process by a special heat-setting process or by modifications made during spinning. Diagram 2–2 compares crimped and uncrimped fibers.

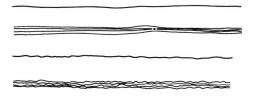 Untextured fiber-filament

Untextured yarn-filament

Textured filament fiber (note slight loss of length)

Textured filament yarn

Stretch-textured fiber (now loses 2/3 length)

 Stretch-textured filament yarn

Diagram 1-2. Fibers and yarns showing varying degrees of crimp.

Materials and Apparatus

    samples of wool, silk, untextured man-made and textured man-made fibers

    linen tester[3]

Procedure

1. Examine each of the fibers under the linen tester.

2. Answer the following questions:

. . . Wool and silk are both natural fibers. Is natural crimp found in wool?____ in silk?____

. . . One man-made fiber sample has had crimp added, the other has not. Describe the difference in the appearance of the two fibers._____

_____

3. Stretch or pull each of the fibers.

. . . Which fibers display more stretch, the crimped or uncrimped fibers? _____

_____

    Why? _____

**5. *Length*

    Fibers of relatively short length measured in inches or centimeters are called *staple* fibers. Long continuous fibers measured in meters or yards are called *filament* fibers. Man-made fibers are manufactured in filament form but can be cut into staple lengths. Man-made fiber manufactured especially for the production of staple is called *tow*.

    Through the examination of yarns, one can determine whether the fibers in a yarn are filament or staple fibers.

Table 1–1 DIFFERENCES BETWEEN FILAMENT AND STAPLE FIBER YARNS	
Filament Fibers in Yarns	**Staple Fibers in Yarns**
Fibers are as long as the yarn	Fibers are shorter than the yarn
When the yarn is untwisted, fibers remain parallel	When the yarn is untwisted, fibers are not all completely parallel
The surface of the yarn is usually smoother	The surface of the yarn appears fuzzier because of the fiber ends
Little or no twist may be used	

[3]See Appendix B for instructions on the use of the linen tester.

Materials

four samples of fabric or yarn, 2″ (5 cm) square or larger

linen tester

pick needle

Procedure

1. Unravel several yarns from the first sample.

2. Untwist the yarn to separate the yarn into fibers. Using the linen tester examine the yarn and fibers and compare them to Table 1–1.

3. Identify the fiber content of the yarn as either staple or filament. Mount a small sample of the fabric in the space provided and label the sample as "filament" or "staple."

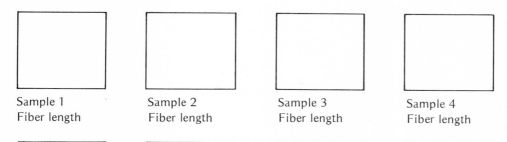

Sample 1
Fiber length

Sample 2
Fiber length

Sample 3
Fiber length

Sample 4
Fiber length

B. Fiber Properties Relating to Performance

*1. Strength

The strength of textile fibers is referred to as their *tenacity*. Tenacity is determined by measuring the force required to rupture or break the fiber. In the textile industry or research laboratory, the tenacity of textile fibers is measured on a breaking strength tester. A number of tests, each one specific to a particular fiber or type of fibers has been established. These tests are published each year in the American Society for Testing Materials *Annual Book of Standards*. These tests provide a reliable, well-controlled measure of tenacity. It is from such tests that the figures for tenacity given in the text or in general reference materials are determined.

The following simple experiment will provide a general comparison of the strength of several different textile fibers. It is *not* a technical test for tenacity or breaking strength.

Materials

four samples each of regular tenacity viscose rayon and nylon filament fibers, at least 6–8″ (15–20 cm) in length

Procedure

1. Hold one of the four viscose samples by each end, grasping the sample tightly.

2. Pull on the sample until it breaks or until you determine that it cannot be broken. Repeat on the other three samples. Be sure to use samples made up of about the same number of fibers.

3. Rate the resistance of the fiber to breaking on the following chart.

4. Repeat steps 1 to 3 with the nylon samples. Be sure to use about the same number of nylon fibers in each sample as were used in the rayon samples.

Chart 1-2 STRENGTH OF SELECTED FIBERS			
Fiber	Check off one:		
	resists breaking	moderate resistance to breaking	breaks readily
Regular tenacity viscose Rayon filament			
Regular tenacity nylon filament			

From this comparison, what conclusion can be drawn as to the relative strength of regular tenacity viscose and nylon filament fiber?_____

*2. *Specific Gravity*

Specific gravity is the density of a fiber in relation to the density of an equal volume of water. A fiber with the same density as water is said to have a specific gravity of one. A fiber with a higher density than water would have a specific gravity of more than one, and a fiber with a lower density than water would have a specific gravity of less than one, in which case it would float on the top of the water.

Materials and Apparatus

two fabric samples each 1" (2.5 cm) square, one of olefin and one of glass fiber
250 ml glass beaker or clear glass tumbler
detergent
water

Procedure

1. Fill the beaker (or glass) with 200 ml of tap water.

2. Add a drop or two of detergent to the water. Agitate to mix the detergent and water.

3. Place both fabric samples in the water. Observe the results and answer the following questions.

. . . Does the glass fabric float or sink? _____

. . . Does the olefin fabric float or sink? _____

. . . Which sample has the higher specific gravity? _____

. . . Does either sample have a specific gravity of less than one?_____

If yes, which one? _____

Why do you draw this conclusion? _____

Look up the specific gravity of each fiber in the text or a reference source: glass

fiber _____ olefin _____

4. *Elongation and Elastic Recovery*

(1) *Elongation* is the ability of fibers to stretch or lengthen. Elastic recovery is the ability of fibers to return to their original length after being stretched. Some fibers, called *elastomeric* fibers, can be stretched to many times their length; others show little ability to be elongated. Special equipment is required to measure elongation. These procedures and tests are reported each year in the *Annual Book of Standards* of the American Society for Testing Materials, Part 33.

Elastic recovery is measured by the ASTM test D 1774, Part 33 of the *Annual Book of Standards*. It too requires special equipment and carefully controlled conditions. Described briefly, the test elongates a test specimen of fiber or fabric to a specified percentage of its length and then allows the test specimen to recover from elongation for a specified period of time.

The length of the recovered specimen is measured, and the percentage of recovery is calculated by the following formula:

$$\frac{\begin{array}{l}\text{original}\\\text{sample}\\\text{length}\end{array} - \left(\begin{array}{l}\text{length of}\\\text{recovered}\\\text{sample}\end{array} - \begin{array}{l}\text{length}\\\text{of original}\\\text{sample}\end{array}\right)}{\text{Original Sample Length}} \times 100$$

Given the following measurements, calculate the percentage of elastic recovery of the following sample:

Original sample length is 100 cm.

Length of recovered sample is 108 cm.

Show your calculations here:

5. *Resilience*

Resilience is the ability of the fiber to spring back to its original position after folding, creasing, or other deformation. There is no specific test for resilience of fibers because the construction of the fabric is often related to resiliency. In order to evaluate fabric resiliency, tests of wrinkle recovery have been devised and a simple demonstration of the concept can be made as follows:

*Materials

     two, 4″ (10 cm) squares of linen fabric without wrinkle-resistant finish

     two 4″ (10 cm) squares of polyester fabric

Procedure

1. Holding a test specimen of linen fabric in the hand, close the fist tightly and hold the fabric inside the closed fist for one minute.

2. At the end of one minute, place the wrinkled fabric on a flat surface. Do not smooth out any creases that have formed.

3. Observe the test specimen to see how wrinkled it became. Compare with the un-wrinkled sample of the same fabric.

4. Allow the fabric to relax for five minutes, then examine it again. Compare it to the unwrinkled sample. Note to what extent the creases have relaxed and the fabric has recovered from wrinkling.

5. Repeat steps 1 to 4 with the polyester fabric.

Questions

. . . Which of the two fabrics was more wrinkled immediately after creasing? _____
_____

. . . Which of the two fabrics showed better recovery from wrinkling after a five-minute

interval?_____

. . . Which of the two fabrics can be said to have better wrinkle recovery?_____
_____

. . . Which of the two fabrics is more resilient?_____
_____

A second, simple test for wrinkle recovery can be performed.

**Materials

two or more specimens of fabrics to be tested measuring 2″ (5 cm) in the warp direction and 2¼″ (6 cm) in the filling direction
a 1-pound weight or a 500-gram weight for each test specimen

Procedure

1. The instructor will identify the fiber content of the test specimens.

2. Fold the test specimen in half in the lengthwise direction, then fold the same specimen in half again on the crosswise direction. (See Diagram 1-3.)

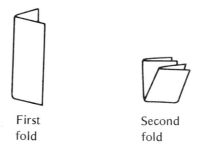

First   Second
fold   fold

Diagram 1-3.
Folding of specimen for wrinkle recovery test.

3. Place the test specimen under the weight for five minutes.

4. Remove the weights. Observe the depth of the creasing. Record the observation on Chart 1-3.

5. Invert the test sample so that the creased edge is upward. (See diagram 1-4.)

Diagram 1-4.
Recovery position for wrinkle recovery specimen.

6. Allow the sample to recover for five minutes, then examine it again to determine whether the fabric has shown any recovery from creasing. Record the observation on Chart 1-3.

Chart 1-3	CREASE RECOVERY OF SELECTED FABRICS					
	Pronounced Creasing	Moderate Creasing	Little Creasing	Recovery from creasing is		
				Minimal	Moderate	Complete
Sample 1 Fiber Content						
Sample 2 Fiber Content						
Other Samples						

In this experiment, which sample showed better resilience?

6. *Absorbency*

Absorbency is the ability of a fiber to absorb or take water into itself. Some fibers are very absorbent and absorb water very quickly; some fibers are less absorbent, absorbing water more slowly; some fibers absorb little or no water. In a textile laboratory the absorbency of textile fibers may be calculated as *moisture regain*. Standardized procedures for determining moisture regain are reported in *ASTM Annual Book of Standards*, part 33, test D629, "Moisture Content or Moisture Regain of Fibers" and D2654, "Moisture Content and Moisture Regain of Textile Materials." The procedure requires that a fiber, yarn, or fabric sample be dried to remove all moisture from within the sample. It is weighed dry, then exposed to conditions of standard temperature and humidity that are 70°F (21.1°C) and 65 per cent relative humidity, for a specified period of time. The sample is reweighed after this exposure, and the difference between the weight when bone dry and the weight when moisture has been returned to the fiber is calculated. The moisture regain figures reported in the text and in reference materials have been determined by the ASTM tests, and a table of moisture regain figures is printed in the ASTM *Annual Book of Standards*, in Parts 32 and 33, Number D1909.

Regain of moisture to the saturated state can also be calculated. The procedure is similar, except that dried fiber, yarn, or fabric is exposed to 100 per cent humidity, and the weight is calculated. The following procedure, although not a technical test because it does not provide for adequate control of temperature and humidity, demonstrates the difference in absorbency between two fabrics each one of which is made from a different fiber.

Experiment 1: Saturation

Materials and apparatus

     one sample of fabric, 4″ (10 cm) square of filament rayon fabric, plain weave
     one sample of fabric, 4″ (10 cm) square of filament nylon fabric, plain weave
     balance for weighing samples
     two watch glasses
     250 ml beaker
     oven
     tongs

Procedure

***1. Dry the sample in an oven at 230°F (110°C) for 30 minutes.

2. Remove the sample from the oven with a pair of tongs, place it on a dry watch glass, and weigh the sample and the watch glass immediately. (If an oven is not available, simply weigh a dry sample of fabric) Record the weight.

3. Fill a 250 ml beaker with tepid water. Holding the sample with tongs, immerse the sample in water for two minutes.

4. Remove the sample from the water with the tongs, and allow water to run off the sample until no more water drips from the sample (at least two minutes).

5. Place the sample on the watch glass and reweigh. Record the weight.

6. The percentage of water absorbed by the fabric can be calculated as follows:

$$\frac{\text{wet weight} - \text{dry weight}}{\text{dry weight}} \times 100 \text{ equals } \% \text{ held at the saturation point}$$

7. Calculate the percentage of moisture held at the saturation point for each sample.

    Rayon: ___ % held

    nylon _____ % held

Questions

... Which sample absorbed more water? _____

... From the moisture regain figures in the text or reference materials determine whether the general absorbency is comparable to that expected for these two fabrics. Explain.

_____
_____
_____

*Experiment 2: Hoop Test of Absorbency

The following test will also provide a general comparison of fabrics made from fibers with differing absorbency. In order to avoid having the fabric structure interfere with the comparison, two fabrics of similar fabric construction must be used.

Materials and Apparatus:

one fabric specimen 8" (20 cm) square of plain weave filament rayon, closely woven

one fabric specimen 8" (20 cm) square of plain weave, filament nylon, closely woven

6" (15 cm) embroidery hoop

eyedropper

stopwatch

Procedure

1. Work with a partner. Place one fabric sample on the hoop, being careful to mount the sample so that it is free of wrinkles.

2. Put the hoop on a flat surface. One person should hold the eyedropper 3/8 inch above the specimen and perpendicular to the specimen. Allow one drop of water to fall on the specimen. When the drop falls onto the sample, the other person should start the timing. With the stopwatch, record the length of time required for the drop of water to be absorbed by the specimen. The water is absorbed at the precise time when the drop can no longer be seen on the surface of the specimen. Record the time.

3. Repeat this test two more times, each time placing the drop in a different area of the fabric. Average the wetting time for this fabric. Record the average.

4. Compare the results:
   rayon: average wetting time:
   nylon: average wetting time:
   good absorbency is considered to require less than five seconds wetting time; poor absorbency is considered to require more than five seconds wetting time.

Questions:

. . . Which sample showed "good" absorbency?_____

Which sample showed "poor" absorbency? _____

. . . Do these results show any similarity to the results of the test for percentage of satura-

tion regain? Explain._____

_____

_____

_____

7. *Electrical Conductivity*

Electrical conductivity is the ability of a fiber to carry or transfer electrical charges. This property can be measured objectively by testing yarns or fabrics with an Electrical

Resistance Meter. Many individuals have had subjective experiences with the electrical conductivity of fabrics: fabrics that cling, shocks received as a result of walking across a carpet made from fibers with poor electrical conductivity, and the sparks that can be seen in a dark room when a synthetic blanket is shaken. Moisture regain characteristics of fibers may have an effect on their electrical conductivity. The moisture regain figures for a number of fibers are listed on the following chart. From reading in the text, determine whether the electrical conductivity of these fibers is considered to be poor or good. Enter this information on the chart.

Chart 1-4	ELECTRICAL CONDUCTIVITY AND MOISTURE REGAIN OF SELECTED FIBERS	
Fiber	Moisture Regain[a]	Electrical Conductivity
Cotton	7–8%	
Rayon	11%	
Nylon	4.5%	
Polyester	0.4%	
Acrylic	1.5%	

[a] ASTM *Annual Book of Standards*, Part 32 or 33, D 1909.

Questions

. . . From the figures on the chart, determine whether good electrical conductivity is related to low moisture regain or higher moisture regain. Explain.

_____

_____

_____

8. *Dimensional Stability*

Dimensional stability results when fibers neither shrink nor stretch. It is important to differentiate between the dimensional stability of fibers and the dimensional stability of fabrics. Although fibers may be dimensionally stable, the fabrics into which they are made may not. As a result of spinning and weaving, or knitting, the fabrics may become stretched. These fabrics will relax during any wetting process, as during cleaning. When relaxed, they return to their true dimensions and exhibit shrinkage. Thus, although the individual fibers do not shrink or stretch, the fabrics into which they are made may show shrinkage or stretching.

Tests for dimensional stability of *fabrics* will be made in Units Three and Five. Tests for dimensional stability of *fibers* require special equipment and skilled laboratory techniques and cannot be carried out in a beginning textile laboratory. The dimensional stability characteristics of each fiber, as distinct from those of fabrics, are discussed in the text.

9. *Effect of Heat, Burning Characteristics*

**(1) Effect of Heat

Fibers react to the application of heat in different ways. Some fibers scorch, some melt, and some are unaffected except at very high temperatures. The following exercise will contrast two fibers with markedly different reactions to heat.

Materials and Apparatus

one 4″ (10 cm) square of cotton and one of acetate fabric

hand iron

ironing board or padded surface

Procedure

1. Set the hand iron at the lowest temperature setting. Preheat for five minutes.

2. Place the iron on a corner of the fabric sample. Hold the iron against the sample for one minute. Observe the effects, if any, such as color change, shrinking, or melting.

3. Increase the temperature to the next setting. Hold the iron against the sample for one minute. Observe the effects, if any.

4. Continue to do this, increasing the heat setting after each application until the fabric is visibly affected by the heat.

5. Record the setting of the iron at which one can see that the fabric is affected. Record the effect of the heat on the fabric.

(Note: hand irons vary in the accuracy of their settings, so this experiment provides a comparison, rather than a precise measure, of the effects of the heat.) Record the data on Chart 1-5.

Chart 1-5	EFFECT OF HEAT ON SELECTED FIBERS	
Fabric	Setting of the Iron at Which the Sample Is Affected	Effect of Heat on the Fabric
Cotton		
Acetate		

**(2) Burning Characteristics

The burning characteristics of fibers vary. These differences in burning characteristics are sometimes used to aid in fiber identification and are important in the evaluation of potential fire hazards from fabrics. In the following test, a few fibers are burned to show how these characteristics may differ.

Materials and Apparatus

bundle of five or six yarns of the following fibers:

nylon

cotton

acrylic

glass

matches

tweezers

candle or Bunsen burner

protected (nonflammable) surface

Procedure

1. Work with a partner. One partner will perform the tests, the other will record the data.

2. Hold the yarns of one fiber in the tweezers. Move the yarns close to the flame, but do not place them in the flame. Note if the yarns melt or shrink away from the flame. Record the results on Chart 1-6.

3. Move the yarns into the flame. Note whether the yarns burn in the flame. Record the results on Chart 1-6.

4. Remove the yarns from the flame very carefully and slowly, noting whether the yarns continue to burn outside the flame. Be certain that the yarns were ignited before making this observation. Record the results on Chart 1-6.

5. Blow out the flame on the yarns if they are still burning. Smell the smoke. (Note: individual differences in the perceptions of odors may exist. Certain fibers have very distinctive odors, others may be more difficult to describe objectively.) Describe the odor on Chart 1-6.

6. Examine the appearance of the ash that remains at the end of the burned yarns. Record the results on Chart 1-6.

Chart 1-6 BURNING CHARACTERISTICS OF SELECTED FIBERS						
Sample	Melts Near Flame	Shrinks from Flame	Burns in Flame	Continues to burn	Odor of Burned Fiber	Appearance of Ash
Nylon						
Cotton						
Acrylic						
Glass						

10. *Resistance to Microorganisms, Insects, Sunlight, and Aging*

Fibers differ in their resistance to environmental conditions. To test such resistance requires either long-term observation or specialized laboratory equipment designed to simulate these conditions. A Fade-Ometer or a carbon arc lamp apparatus can be used to simulate the degradation of fabrics by sunlight. After specified periods of exposure (50 hours in the Fade-Ometer are required to equal one season of use for draperies, for example), the fabrics can be tested for loss of strength. The *ASTM Annual Book of Standards* describes the use of this equipment in test G-25. If the laboratory is equipped with a Fade-Ometer or an equivalent apparatus, the instructor may demonstrate its use.

A test to evaluate the resistance of textiles to insects has also been developed. AATCC Test Method 24-1974 describes this test.

Part 4: CHEMICAL PROPERTIES OF TEXTILE FIBERS

Reference Chapter 2, *Understanding Textiles* or assigned readings in text or reference books.

Each textile fiber has a unique chemical composition. The chemical composition is the means of establishing the generic fiber category to which each fiber belongs. Nevertheless even fibers from the same generic fiber category may exhibit small differences in chemical composition and behavior. In general, however, it is accurate to say that fibers from the same generic fiber category and those from similar natural fiber groups such as the cellulosic and protein fibers exhibit similarities in chemical behavior.

The substances with which fibers come into contact during their manufacturing, finishing, and care are also chemical in nature. For this reason an understanding of the chemical properties of fibers is important not only to the manufacturer and the finisher but also to the consumer. Many of the substances used with textiles are either acid or alkaline in reaction. The reaction of textiles to acids and alkalis or other solvents is often used as a means of identifying unknown textile fibers. Chlorine bleach, an oxidizing agent agent frequently used in the home in order to whiten fabrics, affects some fibers adversely.

The following few simple experiments are intended to contrast the reaction of two fibers to the same chemical substances. *Safety Note*: Activities that utilize chemical substances must be carried out very carefully, as some of these substances are harmful to the eyes, skin, and clothing. The experiments that follow should be carried out only in a laboratory setting under the supervision of an instructor. The following guidelines are important safety precautions.

1. Protect clothing by wearing a laboratory coat or apron.

2. Avoid touching eyes and mouth with hands while handling chemicals. If chemicals spill or splatter on the skin, wash them off at once.

3. Keep hands away from hot or moving parts of testing equipment.

4. Work on protected surfaces.

5. Turn off all equipment immediately after their use.

6. Tie back long hair.

7. In general, work slowly and carefully. Do not leave experimental materials unattended.

The instructor will organize the laboratory and instruct students as to whether they will work individually, or in groups. In some instances, the instructor may demonstrate the procedures.

(1) Experiments: The Effect of Acids on Selected Textile Fibers

The following experiments contrast the effect of acids on two different fibers. Since the effect of acids on fibers may be increased as the temperature of the acid increases, the tests are carried out both at room temperature and at elevated temperatures. Acids may also be strong or weak, mineral or organic. The tests utilize different concentrations and types of acids.

**Test 1*: *The Effect of Strong Mineral Acids at Room Temperature*

Materials and Apparatus
    two 1″ (2.5 cm) squares of fabric, one of cotton, one of polyester
    two watch glasses
    small tongs
    sulfuric acid, 70% solution

Procedure

1. Place a test specimen of cotton on one watch glass and a test specimen of polyester on the other. Cover each specimen with sulfuric acid (70 per cent solution)

2. Observe immediately and note any changes in the specimen. Observe again after five minutes, and every five minutes thereafter until 20 minutes has elapsed. Record any change on Chart 1-7.

3. If the specimen has not dissolved after 20 minutes, rinse thoroughly, using the tongs to hold the specimen. Be careful not to spill any acid on the hands or clothing. Examine the specimen. Pull on the specimen to see if it has been noticeably weakened. Record the results on Chart 1-7.

4. Repeat procedures 1-3 on the second specimen.

Chart 1-7 EFFECT OF ACIDS ON SELECTED TEXTILE FIBERS							
Fibers	Acid	Temperature	Immediate Effect	After five Minutes	After ten Minutes	After fifteen Minutes	After twenty Minutes
Cotton	70% H_2SO_4	room					
Polyester	70% H_2SO_4	room					
Cotton	70% H_2SO_4	100°F (38°C)					
Polyester	70% H_2SO_4	100°F (38°C)					
Cotton	20% H_2SO_4	room					
Polyester	20% H_2SO_4	room					
Cotton	20% H_2SO_4	100°F (38°C)					
Polyester	20% H_2SO_4	100°F (38°C)					
Cotton	vinegar	room					
Polyester	vinegar	room					

***Test 2: *The Effect of Strong Mineral Acids at Elevated Temperatures*

Materials and Apparatus
    two 1″ (2.5 cm) squares of fabric, one of cotton, one of polyester
    Bunsen burner and ring stand or hot plate

250 ml beaker
two test tubes
laboratory thermometer
small tongs
sulfuric acid, 70% solution

Procedure

1. Fill the beaker about 2/3 full of water. Place over heat. Heat until the water temperature reaches 100.4°F or 38°C. Use the laboratory thermometer to check the temperature.

2. Place each test specimen in a test tube. Add enough sulfuric acid solution to cover the specimens.

3. Place the test tubes in the heated water bath. Allow the test tubes to heat for three minutes, then observe the specimens. Note any change in the specimens.

4. Observe after five minutes, and every five minutes thereafter until 20 minutes has elapsed. Record any changes in the specimens on Chart 1-7.

5. If the specimens have not dissolved after 20 minutes, remove them with the tongs, and rinse thoroughly, being careful not to spill any acid on the hands or clothes. Examine the specimens. Pull on the specimens to see if they have been noticeably weakened. Record the results on Chart 1-7.

**Test 3: *The Effect of Weak Mineral Acids at Room Temperature*

Materials and Apparatus
    two 1″ (2.5 cm) squares of fabric, one of cotton, one of polyester
    watch glasses
    tongs
    sulfuric acid, 20% solution

Procedure

1. Follow the procedures outlined in Test 1: The Effect of Strong Mineral Acids at Room Temperature, except use 20 per cent sulfuric acid solution.

2. Record the results on Chart 1-7.

***Test 4: *The Effect of Weak Mineral Acids at Elevated Temperatures*

Materials and Apparatus:
    two 1″ (2.5 cm) squares of fabric, one of cotton, one of polyester
    Bunsen burner and ring stand or hot plate
    two test tubes
    laboratory thermometer
    small tongs
    sulfuric acid, 20% solution

Procedure

1. Follow the procedures outlined in Test 2: The Effect of Strong Mineral Acids at Elevated Temperatures, except use 20 per cent sulfuric acid solution.

2. Record the results on Chart 1-7.

**Test 5*: The Effect of Organic Acids at Room Temperature*

Materials and Apparatus
   two 1″ (2.5 cm) squares of fabric, one of cotton, one of polyester
   two watch glasses
   small tongs
   vinegar

Procedure

1. Follow the procedures outlined in Test 1: The Effect of Strong Mineral Acids at Room Temperature, except use vinegar, full strength.

2. Record the results on Chart 1-7.

Questions

. . . Did any of the samples show a consistent pattern of resistance to destruction by acids. If so, which one(s)? _____

_____

_____

. . . Did any of the samples show a consistent pattern of destruction or damage at certain temperatures but not others? If so, which one(s)? _____

_____

_____

. . . As a result of these tests, would manufacturers of either cotton or polyester have to take special precautions with chemical finishing of the fabric with materials that had a strongly acid reaction? If so, why? _____

_____

_____

_____

_____

(2) Experiments: The Effect of alkalis on selected textile fibers.

Test 1: The Effect of Alkalis, Room Temperature

Materials and Apparatus
   two 1″ (2.5 cm) squares of fabric, one of cotton, one of silk
   two watch glasses
   small tongs
   sodium hydroxide or potassium hydroxide, 5% solution

Procedure

1. Follow the procedures outlined in Test 1: The Effect of Strong Acids at Room Temperature, except use 5 per cent sodium hydroxide or potassium hydroxide.

2. Record the results on Chart 1-8.

Test 2: The Effect of Hot Alkalis

Materials and Apparatus:
    two 1″ (2.5 cm) squares of fabric, one of silk and one of cotton
    hot plate or Bunsen burner and ring stand
    two 250 ml beakers
    two watch glasses
    sodium hydroxide or potassium hydroxide, 5% solution

Procedures

1. Place each test specimen in a beaker. Cover the specimen with 25 ml of sodium hydroxide or potassium hydroxide solution.

2. Cover each beaker with a watch glass to prevent evaporation of the sodium hydroxide solution.

3. Bring each solution to a boil. Observe each specimen as soon as the solution comes to a boil. Note any change in the specimens. Record the results on Chart 1-8.

4. Continue boiling the solution for five minutes.

5. Observe each specimen and record the results on Chart 1-8.

6. If the specimen has not dissolved, remove it from solution with the tongs and rinse thoroughly, being careful not to spill any of the alkali on the hands or clothing. Pull on the specimen to see if it has been noticeably weakened. Record the results on Chart 1-8.

Chart 1-8 EFFECT OF ALKALIS ON SELECTED TEXTILE FIBERS							
Fibers	Chemicals	Temperature	Immediate Effect	After five Minutes	After ten Minutes	After fifteen Minutes	After twenty Minutes
cotton	NaOH or KOH	room					
silk	NaOH or KOH	room					
cotton	NaOH or KOH	boiling					
silk	NaOH or KOH	boiling					

Questions

. . . Many laundry detergents have alkaline substances added to improve their cleaning effectiveness. As a result of this test what conclusions can be drawn about the advisability of laundering silk fabrics with strongly alkaline detergents at high temperatures for long periods of time? Why? _____

_____

_____

. . . Would the same be true of laundering cotton fabrics under the same conditions?

Why?_____

_____

_____

Compare the reaction of cotton to acids and alkalis. _____

_____

_____

Test 3: The Effect of Chlorine Bleach on Selected Textile Fibers

Materials and Apparatus

two fabric samples, 1″ (2.5 cm) square, one of silk and one of nylon

Bunsen burner and ring stand or hot plate

laboratory thermometer

250 ml beaker

small tongs

chlorine bleach

water

Procedure

1. Cut off one small corner of the silk specimen in order to distinguish it from the nylon specimen.

2. In a beaker dilute 25 ml of commercial liquid chlorine bleach with 125 ml of distilled water.

3. Add test specimens to the solution.

4. Place the beaker over heat, and heat to temperature of 105-115°F (40-45°C). Maintain this heat for 20 minutes.

5. After 20 minutes, remove the specimens from the bleach. Rinse well and dry samples.

6. Examine the specimens for any effect on fibers. Pull on the specimen to see if it is visibly weakened. (Do not be concerned about any color change, but determine whether the specimen seems degraded or weakened as a result of bleaching.)

Questions

. . . From this experiment, what can be concluded about the advisability of laundering silk fabrics with chlorine bleach? Why?_____

_____

. . . What can be concluded about the effect of chlorine bleach on nylon fabrics?

_____

Test 4: The Effects of Selected Solvents on Textile Fibers

Some fibers are adversely affected by specific chemical substances. Acetone is one substance that may adversely affect some fibers.

Materials and Apparatus
    two fabric samples, 1″ (2.5 cm) squares, one of cotton, one of acetate
    two watch glasses
    tongs
    acetone

Procedure

1. Unravel a few yarns from the sample. Place the yarns on a watch glass.

2. Cover with acetone.

3. Observe at once and note any change in the fabric samples.

4. Observe after five minutes. Note any change in the yarns.

5. If the yarns have not dissolved, pick them up with the tongs and rinse them thoroughly. Pull on the yarns to see if they have been noticeably weakened.

    Record the results in the spaces provided.

    Effect of acetone on cotton _____

    Effect of acetone on acetate _____

Question

. . . Some nail polish removers contain acetone. What precautions should be taken in using such a product? _____

_____

_____

Use and Care of Textiles

Although these experiments were performed on a few selected fibers in order to demonstrate particular properties of the fibers, it should be remembered that each generic fiber grouping has its own unique characteristics. It is these characteristics that make the fiber suitable for use in particular end products. The fiber properties also determine the specific care procedures necessary to maintain fabrics made from each type of fiber. The preceding activities and those that follow in the next section are, therefore, related to the determination of appropriate uses for fibers and to the care they require when they are made into a specific end product.

Part 5: GENERIC TEXTILE FIBERS

References Chapters 3 to 12, *Understanding Textiles* or assigned readings in text or reference books.

Procedure

1. Read the chapters dealing with each of the specific generic fiber groupings under study. Fibers for which evaluations will be carried out include

    cotton

    linen

    regular viscose rayon

    acetate

    wool

    silk

    glass fiber

    nylon

    polyester

    acrylic

    modacrylic

    olefin

    spandex

2. The instructions that follow are for experiments and/or tests to be performed on each fiber. The instructor will designate those activities that are to be carried out and may omit or modify others. A master fabric sample 14" (35 cm) warp X 16" (40 cm) filling will be provided to test each fiber. Test specimens for the following experiments will be cut from the master sample. (See Diagram 1-5.)

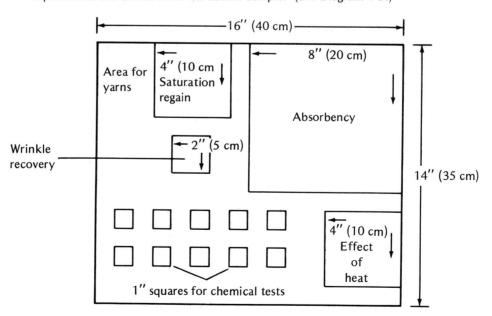

Diagram 1-5.
Plan for cutting of test specimens for generic fiber tests.

3. Enter the data derived from these activities on Chart 1-9. When completed, this chart will provide a basis for comparing different generic fiber categories and their properties.

A. General Information

The instructor will provide information about the sample of fabric made from each fiber on which tests will be performed, including fiber content and other available information such as the trademark or special finishes that have been applied. Enter this information on Chart 1-9. Mount a 1″ (2.5 cm) square swatch of the fabric in the space provided on the chart.

B. Fiber Characteristics Relating to Appearance

Materials and Apparatus
    undyed, unbleached fiber sample[4]
    master fabric sample
    microscope and prepared slide of the longitudinal view of the fiber or photomicrographs of the fiber
    light source

Procedure

1. Examine an undyed, unbleached sample of the fiber. Record the color on Chart 1-9.

2. Examine the undyed, unbleached sample under a light source. Indicate whether the sample has low, moderate, or high luster. From the test determine whether the fiber can be delustered. Record this information on Chart 1-9.

3. Examine a prepared slide of the fiber and/or a photomicrograph from the text or a reference book. Describe the appearance of the longitudinal view and the appearance of the cross-sectional view on the chart.

4. From the text determine whether the fiber is found or manufactured in filament, staple, or tow forms. Record this information on the chart. Unravel a yarn from the large master sample of the fabric. Untwist the yarn and determine whether the fiber in this fabric sample is filament or staple. Record on Chart 1-9.

C. General Characteristics of the Fiber Relating to Behavior

(1) Strength

Materials and Apparatus
    master test sample

---

[4]This may be a part of a display provided by the instructor or where indicated by the instructor may be unraveled from the master fabric sample.

Fiber	Cotton	Linen	Viscose Rayon	Acetate	Wool	Silk
Sample of Fabric						
A. Special treatments or finishes given the fabric sample						
B. Characteristics of the fiber: Appearance (1) Color of undyed sample (2) Luster						
(3) Microscopic appearance: Longitude Cross-section	———	———	———	———	———	———
(4) Fiber length available in this sample is	———	———	———	———	———	———
C. Characteristics of the Fiber: Behavior (1) Strength, general evaluation (2) Tenacity-dry Tenacity-wet						
(3) Specific gravity						
(4) Elongation and elastic recovery						
(5) Resilience						
(6) Absorbency: Moisture regain:						
(7) Electrical conductivity						
(8) Dimensional stability						

Chart 1-9

Glass Fiber	Nylon	Polyester	Acrylic	Modacrylic	Olefin	Spandex
—	—	—	—	—	—	—
—	—	—	—	—	—	—

Chart 1-9 (cont.)	Cotton	Linen	Viscose Rayon	Acetate	Wool	Silk
(9) Effect of heat: temperature setting at which fabric is affected: effect of heat	_____	_____	_____	_____	_____	_____
Burning characteristics a. melts near flame b. shrinks from flame c. burns in flame d. continues to burn e. appearance of ash	_____ _____ _____ _____ _____	_____ _____ _____ _____ _____	_____ _____ _____ _____ _____	_____ _____ _____ _____ _____	_____ _____ _____ _____ _____	_____ _____ _____ _____ _____
(10) Resistance to microorganisms, etc.						
D. Chemical Properties (1) Effect of acids: a. concentrated, mineral room temperature b. concentrated hot mineral c. weak mineral room temperature d. weak, hot mineral e. organic (2) Effect of alkalis: 5% NaOH or KOH, room temperature 5% NaOH or KOH, boiling (3) Effect of Chlorine bleach (4) Effect of acetone	_____ _____ _____ _____ _____ _____ _____	_____ _____ _____ _____ _____ _____ _____	_____ _____ _____ _____ _____ _____ _____	_____ _____ _____ _____ _____ _____ _____	_____ _____ _____ _____ _____ _____ _____	_____ _____ _____ _____ _____ _____ _____
E. Special Care Required for Fabrics Made from This Fiber						
F. Major End Uses of the Fabrics Made from This Fiber						

Glass Fiber	Nylon	Polyester	Acrylic	Modacrylic	Olefin	Spandex
—	—	—	—	—	—	—
—	—	—	—	—	—	—
—	—	—	—	—	—	—
—	—	—	—	—	—	—
—	—	—	—	—	—	—
—	—	—	—	—	—	—
—	—	—	—	—	—	—
—	—	—	—	—	—	—
—	—	—	—	—	—	—
—	—	—	—	—	—	—
—	—	—	—	—	—	—
—	—	—	—	—	—	—
—	—	—	—	—	—	—

Procedure

1. Unravel a yarn from the master test sample. Untwist the yarn to obtain a few fibers. Where possible, obtain fiber samples five to six inches in length.

2. Hold the fibers tightly between the thumb and forefinger of each hand. Pull on the fibers until they break or until it is certain that they will not break.

3. Rate the resistance of the fibers to breaking as either

. . . resists breaking

. . . moderate resistance to breaking

. . . breaks easily

Record the rating on Chart 1-9.

(2) Check the tenacity rating given for this fiber in the wet and dry state. If several ratings are given, use the rating for regular tenacity fibers. Record this figure on Chart 1-9.

(3) Determine the specific gravity of the fiber from the text or a reference book and record on Chart 1-9.

(4) Elongation and Elastic Recovery

Elastic recovery ratings of fibers are influenced by the percentage of extension, the humidity, and other factors and show considerable variation from test to test. From the text determine the general elongation and elastic recovery characteristics of this fiber and record this general description in the space provided on Chart 1-9.

(5) Resilience

Materials and Apparatus

    test specimen 2″ (5 cm) in the warp and 2¼″

    (6 cm) in the filling

    a 1-pound weight or 500-gram weight

Procedure

1. Fold the test specimen in half in the shorter dimension, then fold the specimen in half again in the longer dimension.

2. Place the test specimen under the weight for five minutes.

3. Remove the weights and observe the depth of the creasing. Record the observation on Chart 1-9.

4. Invert the sample so that the creased edges are upward.

5. Allow the sample to recover for five minutes, then examine again to determine whether the fabric has shown any recovery from creasing. Record the observation on Chart 1-9. (Note: Fabric construction will have an effect on crease recovery, so that this test will provide only a general comparison.)

(6) Absorbency

Using the procedures for experiments 1 and 2 on pages 16, 17, fabrics representing each generic fiber can be tested for absorbency. However, fabric construction and wicking (the spread of water along the outer surface of the yarn or fiber) can result in deceptive results for some fibers.

Obtain moisture regain figures from the text or reference materials and record on Chart 1-9.

(7) Electrical Conductivity

Determine from the reading in the text whether the electrical conductivity of this fiber is poor or good. Record on Chart 1-9.

(8) Dimensional Stability

Fabric and yarn structure are so closely related to dimensional stability that one must distinguish between dimensional stability of the fabric and dimensional stability of the fiber. From the text determine the dimensional stability characteristics of this *fiber*. Record on Chart 1-9.

(9) Effect of Heat and Burning Characteristics

Effect of heat

Materials and Apparatus

    4" (10 cm) square sample of fabric
    hand iron
    ironing board or padded surface

Procedure

1. Set the hand iron at the lowest temperature setting. Preheat for five minutes.

2. Place the iron on a corner of the fabric sample. Hold the iron against the sample for one minute. Observe the effects, if any, such as color change, shrinking, or melting.

3. Increase the temperature to the next setting. Hold the iron against the sample for one minute. Observe the effects, if any. Continue to do this increasing the heat setting after each application until the fabric is visibly affected by the heat.

4. Record the setting of the iron at which the fabric is affected and the effect of the heat on Chart 1-9.

Burning characteristics

Materials and Apparatus

    bundle of five or six yarns from the master test sample
    tweezers
    Bunsen burner or candle and matches
    protected, nonflammable surface

Procedure

1. Work with a partner. One partner will perform the tests, the other will record the data.

2. Hold the yarns in the tweezers. Move them close to the flame, but do not place them in the flame. Note if the yarns melt or shrink away from the flame. Record results on Chart 1-9.

3. Move the yarns into the flame. Note whether the yarns burn in the flame. Record the results on Chart 1-9.

4. Remove the yarns from the flame very carefully and slowly, noting whether the yarns continue to burn outside the flame. Be certain that the yarns were ignited before making this observation. Record the results on Chart 1-9.

5. Blow out the flame on the yarns if they are still burning. Examine the appearance of the ash that remains at the end of the burned yarn. Record on Chart 1-9.

(10) Resistance to Microorganisms, Insects, Sunlight, and Aging.

From the text determine whether any of these conditions have a negative effect on this fiber. Record in the space provided on Chart 1-9.

D. Chemical Properties of Fibers

If time and laboratory facilities permit, carry out the experiments outlined on pages 21 through 27 on specimens cut from the master test sample. Record the results on Chart 1-9. If these experiments cannot be performed, information about the effects of these chemicals can be obtained through readings in the text and reference materials provided by the instructor.

E. Special Care Required for Fabrics Made from This Fiber

Some of the care requirements of textile products are determined by the characteristics of the fiber. Others are related to the construction of the yarns and fabrics. Outline on Chart 1-9 the important considerations that are related to fiber properties in caring for fabrics made from this fiber. (See the text for reference.)

F. Major End Uses

From the text determine the major end uses for this fiber. List them in the space provided on Chart 1-9.

UNIT TWO

Yarns

PART 1: YARN CONSTRUCTION

Reference Chapter 13, *Understanding Textiles* or assigned readings in text or reference books.

Yarns are composed of one or more fibers, either staple or filament. In order to hold staple fibers together in the yarn, fibers must be twisted together. Filament yarns may be made from one filament (monofilament) or many filaments (multifilament). Filament yarns are generally given some twist, but the degree of twist may be either very low or very high.

(1) Hand Spinning

Before spinning was mechanized, yarns were spun by hand using a drop spindle. A demonstration of this technique by the instructor may aid in the understanding of how staple fibers can be twisted together in order to form a yarn. Students can also attempt to spin a small length of yarn following the demonstration.

Materials and Apparatus

washed fleece wool
24 inch (61 cm) length of wool starter yarn
drop spindle
pair of wool cards

Procedure

1. Tease or fluff a handful of the wool.

2. Draw fibers evenly into the teeth of the left-hand card.

3. Card fibers until they lie parallel and impurities are removed by drawing the right card across the left card; the handles of the cards move in opposite directions.

4. Turn both handles toward the floor and roll up the carded fibers, making a *rolag* or *sliver.*

5. Place a "starter yarn" on the drop spindle. (See Diagram 2-1.) Winding several turns, pass below the whorl (wheel), then make a half-hitch into the notch at the top of the stick.

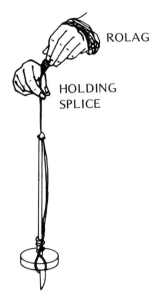

ROLAG

HOLDING
SPLICE

Diagram 2-2.

Placing the starter yarn on the drop spindle and splicing on
the rolag.

6. Splice the rolag onto the end of the starter yarn.

7. The spinning involves two actions: (1) turning or twisting of the spindle while (2) drawing a few fibers from the rolag to receive the twist that is induced by the turning of the spindle. The success of the yarn depends on both steps being co-ordinated: the twist being induced as fibers are drawn from the rolag—the more fiber drawn, the larger is the yarn.

8. When a long yarn has been spun—the spindle arriving at floor level—the spinning is stopped, the yarn is freed from the spindle, and the new yarn is wound onto the spindle stick above the whorl, ready for the next length of yarn to be started. For more detailed instructions and illustrations see R. Castino, *Spinning and Dyeing the Natural Way* (New York: Van Nostrand-Reinhold Company, 1974), pp. 40–43, 47–49.

*(2) Distinguishing Filament from Staple Yarns

Characteristics of Filament Yarns	Characteristics of Staple Yarns
Surface of the yarn is usually smooth.	Surface of the yarn is more fuzzy.
Yarns may be less tightly twisted.	Yarns will have higher twist.
Fibers will be as long as the yarn.	Fibers will be shorter than the yarn.
When untwisted, the yarn will not pull apart.	When untwisted, the yarn will pull apart.
Fibers will be parallel.	Fibers may not be completely parallel.

Materials and Apparatus

　　　six samples of fabric, 1″ (2.5 cm) in the warp by 3″ (8 cm) in the filling

　　　　　　　　　　　　　　or

　　　six samples of yarn 3″ (8 cm) long

　　　linen tester

Procedure

1. Select a yarn or take a fabric sample and unravel several yarns from the filling direction—the 3″ (8 cm) dimension.

2. Untwist the yarn. Examine the fibers to determine their length and whether they are exactly parallel or somewhat randomly positioned.

3. Examine the yarn surface and compare it to the description previously given. Determine whether it is a filament or staple yarn.

4. Trim and mount the sample of fabric or yarn in the space provided (on the following chart.)

Identify the sample as having a filament or staple yarn in the warp.

5. Examine the other five samples following the same procedure.

Sample mounting	Sample mounting	Sample mounting
Warp is filament or staple:	Warp is filament or staple:	Warp is filament or staple:
_____	_____	_____
Sample mounting	Sample mounting	Sample mounting
Warp is filament or staple:	Warp is filament or staple:	Warp is filament or staple:
_____	_____	_____

*(3) Distinguishing Carded from Combed Yarns

Yarns made from staple fibers may be carded or combed. Carded wool yarns are called *woolen yarns*; combed wool yarns are called *worsted yarns.*

Characteristics of Carded Yarns

Surface is fuzzier, has more fiber ends.
Diameter of yarn is somewhat irregular.
Twist is medium to low.
Yarn is usually larger in diameter.
Yarns are composed of varying
   fiber lengths

Characteristics of Combed Yarns

Surface is smoother, has fewer fiber ends.
Diameter of yarn is more even.
Twist may be medium to high.
Yarn is usually finer.
Yarns are composed of more uniform
   and longer lengths.

Materials and Apparatus
   six samples of wool and/or cotton fabric
   1″ (2½ cm) in the warp by 3″ (8 cm) in the filling
   linen tester

Procedure

1. Unravel several filling yarns from a sample.

2. Examine the yarn surface with the linen tester to see whether it is smooth or fuzzy.

3. Examine the yarn to see if the diameter seems fairly even throughout its length or whether it is more uneven.

4. Examine the yarn to see if it has relatively high or low twist.

5. Examine the yarn to determine whether it is thick or fairly fine.

6. Compare the results of your observation to the list of characteristics for carded and combed yarns. Trim the sample to a length of 1¼ inches (3 cm) in the filling and mount in the space provided. In the space provided identify the filling yarn as carded or combed.

7. Examine the five other samples following the same procedure.

Sample mounting

Sample mounting

Sample mounting

Filling yarn is
carded or combed:

Filling yarn is
carded or combed:

Filling yarn is
carded or combed:

_____

_____

_____

Sample mounting	Sample mounting	Sample mounting

Filling yarn is carded or combed: _____

Filling yarn is carded or combed: _____

Filling yarn is carded or combed: _____

*PART 2: DETERMINING THE DIRECTION OF YARN TWIST

(1) Read the section on *S* and *Z twist* in the text. This concept can be illustrated in the following way.

Materials

      small bundle of absorbent cotton fiber or cotton batting
      colored marker

Procedure

1. Separate the cotton fiber into two bundles.

2. With a colored marker make a line of color down the center of each bundle.

3. Hold the fiber at the upper edge of the line between the thumb and forefinger of the left hand and the lower edge by the thumb and forefinger of the right hand. Rotate the fiber to the right with the left hand. The colored line will take a diagonal direction similar to the center bar in a Z.

4. Take the second bunch of fibers and suspend them from the thumb and forefinger of the left hand to the thumb and forefinger of the right hand. Rotate the fiber to the left with the upper left hand. The line you have made will take a diagonal direction similar to the center bar of the S.

5. Right-hand twist results in a *Z twist*. Left-hand twist results in an *S twist*.

(2) Identifying the Direction of Yarn Twist

Materials

      Samples 2'' (5 cm) square of six fabrics for twist identification or six samples of yarn at least 2'' (5 cm) in length
      linen tester

Procedure

1. Unravel a yarn from the fabric sample or use one of the single yarn samples.

2. Place the yarn beside the diagram provided, diagram 2.2.

3. Examine the yarn through a linen tester.

4. Determine whether the line of the twist in the yarn follows the direction of the bar of the S diagram or the bar of the Z diagram.

5. Mount the sample in the space provided, and identify the sample as having an S or a Z twist.

6. Repeat for the other five samples.

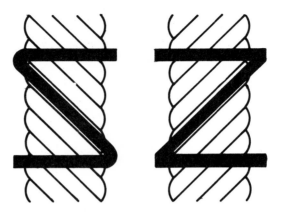

Diagram 2-2.
S and Z twist.

CHART 2-1 S AND Z TWIST					
	Check one:			Check one:	
Sample	S twist	Z twist	Sample	S twist	Z twist
1.			4.		
2.			5.		
3.			6.		

*(3) Twist in Ply Yarns

In some fabrics, two or more yarns are twisted together to make one yarn. Yarns made from two or more yarns twisted together are called *ply yarns*. In a ply yarn, the ply twist can be given an S twist, whereas individual plies would be given a Z twist. This creates a more stable yarn.

Materials
   sample of ply yarn, 4″ (10 cm) long
   linen tester

Procedure

1. Examine the twist of the ply yarn under the linen tester. Is it an S or a Z twist?_____

2. Untwist the ply yarn into its several plies. Examine each ply with the linen tester. What is the direction of the twist in each ply? ply 1 _____ ply 2 _____ other plies _____

PART 3: TYPES OF YARNS

*(1) Yarns are classified by parts. (See Diagram 2-3.) Yarns may have one or more parts.

Single   3-ply   3 cord
Z-twist   S-twist   Z-twist

Diagram 2-3.
Single, ply, and cord yarns.

1. A *single yarn* is made from either filament or staple fibers and when untwisted will separate into the fiber components.

2. A *ply yarn* is made from two or more single yarns that have been twisted together. When untwisted it will separate into single yarns.

3. A *cord yarn* is made from two or more ply yarns twisted together. When untwisted it will separate into ply yarns.

Materials
    three yarn samples: one single, one ply, one cord

Procedure

1. Untwist one end of each yarn sample. Determine whether the sample is a single, ply or cord yarn by examining the form of the untwisted parts—fibers, single yarns or ply yarns.

2. Mount these samples. Label them as either single, ply, or cord yarns.

Sample 1   Sample 2   Sample 3

type of yarn: type of yarn: type of yarn:

_____   _____   _____

**(2) Novelty Yarns

Yarns may be classified as *simple* or *novelty* yarns. Simple yarns are those with uniform size, even twist, and regular surface. Novelty yarns or complex yarns are made to create interesting decorative effects. Simple yarns may be made in single, ply, or cord form. Simple and novelty yarns may be of these same forms but may possess uneven thickness, twist variation along the length or irregular surface effects.

Materials

a set of fabric swatches, each 2″ (5 cm) in the warp by 3″ (8 cm) in the filling

linen tester

Procedure

1. Examine each fabric. Unravel a few yarns from each sample and untwist them. Examine the structure of the yarn, and then determine to which of the following novelty yarn classifications it belongs. Fasten a sample of the fabric in the place beside the novelty yarn it illustrates. Note that novelty yarns may be mixed with simple yarns in fabrics when a decorative effect is desired.

(1) bouclé

. . . ply yarn

. . . effect yarn forms *irregular* loops around base yarn or yarns

. . . another yarn binds or ties the effect yarn to the base

(2) ratiné

. . . ply yarn, similar to bouclé

. . . loops spaced *evenly* along the base yarn

(3) flake yarn or flock yarn

. . . loosely twisted yarns held in place either by (a) base yarn as it twists or (b) third, binder yarn

(4) nub yarn (also known as knop, spot, or knot yarns)

. . . ply yarn

. . . effect yarn twisted around base yarn a number of times in small area to form enlarged bump or "nub"

. . . binder yarn may be used to hold nubs in place

. . . nubs may be at regular or irregular intervals

. . . nubs may be a different color than the base yarn

(5) slub yarn

. . . single or ply yarn

. . . staple fibers

. . . slub created by varying twist in yarn, allowing areas of looser twist to be created

... irregular in diameter

... slub is same color as rest of fabric

... slub cannot be pulled out without damaging fabric

(6) thick and thin yarn

... similar in appearance to the slub

... made from filament fibers with areas of varying twist

(7) snarl yarn

... ply yarn

... varying tension in plys allows effect yarn to form alternating *unclosed* loops on either side of base yarn

(8) spiral or corkscrew yarn

... two-ply yarn with one ply soft and heavy, the other fine

... heavy yarn winds around the fine one

(9) core spun yarn

... central core of one fiber

... second fiber wrapped or twisted around core to form outer layer

*(3) Textured Yarns

Man-made fibers can have texture added in a variety of ways. Texturing may be done in order to produce fabrics with greater bulk or opacity, or to provide stretch. Texturing also helps to decrease pilling.

Materials and Apparatus

four samples of fabrics made from textured yarns, each sample 2″ (5 cm) in the warp by 3″ (8 cm) in the filling. (The instructor will identify the texturing process used or the trademark of the yarn.)

linen tester

pencil

ruler

sheet of unlined paper

Procedure

1. On the chart provided, record the name of the texturing process or the trademark of the yarn used for each sample.

2. Unravel a few of the textured yarns from one fabric sample. Examine the yarns with the linen tester and describe the appearance of the yarn on Chart 2-2.

3. Place the fabric sample on a blank sheet of paper. Trace around the sample with a pencil.

4. Stretch the fabric in the filling direction. Mark and measure the size of the stretched sample. Calculate the amount of stretch by this formula.

$$\frac{\text{Size after stretching} - \text{size before stretching}}{\text{Size before stretching}} \times 100 = \% \text{ of stretch}$$

5. Record this information on Chart 2-2. Mount a sample of the fabric on the chart.

6. Repeat steps 3 to 5 for the lengthwise direction.

7. Repeat steps 2 and 6 for each of the other fabric samples.

CHART 2-2 TEXTURED YARNS				
Sample of Fabric	Trademark or Texturing Process (if known)	Appearance of Yarn	Percentage of Stretch in Length	Percentage of Stretch in Width

Questions

... From the results of the stretching evaluation, list those textured yarns examined in this experiment that seem to have, as a major effect, the provision of stretch.

... From the results of the stretching evaluation, list those textured yarns examined in this experiment that seem to have, as a major effect, the provision of bulk without stretch.

PART 4: YARN ANALYSIS

As a summary activity, samples of fabric can be analyzed to determine the types of yarns they contain. Many fabrics use combinations of different yarns in order to achieve decorative effects. Be sure to unravel a number of yarns from both the warp and the filling in order to ascertain that all of the different yarn types have been identified.

Materials and Apparatus

four fabric samples, 2″ (5 cm) in the warp by 3″ (8 cm) in the filling

linen tester

Procedure

1. Unravel several yarns from the warp direction. Determine how many different yarn types have been used in the warp. When more than one type of yarn has been used, analyze each different type of yarn from the warp. Record the data on Chart 2-3.

2. Untwist the yarn. Determine whether the yarn is staple or filament. Record on Chart 2-3.

3. If the yarn is staple, determine whether the yarn is carded or combed. Record on Chart 2-3.

4. Determine whether the yarn is single, ply, or cord. Record on Chart 2-3.

5. Determine whether the yarn is simple or novelty. Record on Chart 2-3.

6. If the yarn is novelty, determine the type of novelty yarn. Record on Chart 2-3.

7. Mount a sample of the fabric in the space provided on Chart 2-3.

8. Repeat steps 2 to 7 for each warp yarn.

9. Repeat steps 1 to 8 using filling yarns instead of warp yarns.

CHART 2-3 YARN ANALYSIS

		Filament or Staple	Carded or Combed	Single or Ply	Novelty or Simple	If Novelty, Type of Novelty
Sample 1	Warp 1st yarn					
	others					
	Filling 1st yarn					
	others					
Sample 2	Warp 1st yarn					
	others					
	Filling 1st yarn					
	others					

		Filament or Staple	Carded or Combed	Single or Ply	Novelty or Simple	If Novelty, Type of Novelty
Sample 3	Warp 1st yarn					
	others					
	Filling 1st yarn					
	others					
Sample 4	Warp 1st yarn					
	others					
	Filling 1st yarn					
	others					

UNIT THREE

Fabric Construction

PART 1: INTRODUCTION

(1) Fabric Face and Fabric Back

When fabrics are made into an end product, one side of the fabric is treated as the face side (sometimes called the fashion side or "right" side) and the other is treated as the back (or "wrong") side. The characteristics of the face side and the back side are usually sufficiently distinct that one can identify the sides through examination. There are, however, some fabrics in which the face and back are virtually indistinguishable and the fabrics are reversible.

Characteristics of the Face

The face is usually smoother and more lustrous.

In printed fabrics, the print will usually be clearer and brighter on the face.

When special finishes that affect the appearance of fabrics are applied, the finish is generally applied to, or more pronounced on, the face.

In some weaves, i.e., satin and some twills, the floats of the weave are located on the face. In fancy weaves the design may be clear on the face but not on the back.

Characteristics of the Back

Knots and imperfections are generally found on the back.

In printed fabrics, the print will be less distinct and duller on the back.

Materials and Apparatus

    four samples fabric, 2″ (5 cm) in the warp and 3″ (8 cm) in the filling
    linen tester

Procedure

1. Examine each of the samples. Determine which is the face and which is the back.
2. Mount the samples face up in the space provided.

Sample 1   Sample 2

Sample 3   Sample 4

(2) Fabric Top and Bottom

    Some fabrics have a direction or a "top" and "bottom" on the face side, others do not. Corduroy is one such fabric. The difference in appearance results from the difference in light reflectance caused when the pile of the fabric is brushed in one direction. Other fabrics may have a top and a bottom because of a design that runs in only one direction. In constructing products from this type of fabric, care must be taken that all pieces of the product are cut in the same direction, otherwise different sections of the product will appear different in color or design. Types of fabrics with top and bottom are

    pile fabrics, such as corduroy, velvet, velveteen, velour

    satin

    fabrics with special finishes, such as napped or flocked finishes

    some knits

one-directional prints

unbalanced plaids

one-directional woven designs, such as brocades or damasks

Materials

two identical samples of corduroy, each 2″ (5 cm) in the warp and 3″ (8 cm) in the filling

Procedure

1. Take a sample of corduroy. Place it on a flat surface that is well lighted. Lightly run the index finger from the top of the sample to the bottom. Then run the finger from the bottom to the top.
   . . . What difference can you feel? _____

2. Place the second sample on the tabletop beside the first. Place one sample so that the "smooth" direction is toward you, and place the other sample so that the "rough" direction is toward you.
   . . . Can you observe any difference in appearance? What is it? _____

3. Mount the samples with the pile of each sample running in opposite directions.

Corduroy Samples

Space is provided for mounting additional samples of one-directional fabrics.

(3) Identifying Warp and Filling Yarns in Woven Fabrics

Materials and Apparatus
      four samples of fabric, each 3″ (8 cm) square
      linen tester
      pick needle

Procedure

1. Read the material in the following table that lists the differences between warp and filling yarns.

TABLE 3-1 DIFFERENCES BETWEEN WARP AND FILLING YARNS

Warp Yarns	Filling Yarns
Warp yarns run parallel to the selvage	Filling yarns run perpendicular to the selvage
Warp yarns are usually thinner	Filling yarns may be thicker
Warp yarns are usually stronger	Filling yarns may be weaker
Warp yarns usually have more twist	Filling yarns may have less twist
In an unbalanced weave, warp yarns are usually greater in number	In an unbalanced weave, filling yarns are usually less in number
When both filament and staple yarns are used in one fabric, filament yarns are usually warp yarns.	When both filament and staple yarns are used in one fabric, staple yarns are usually filling yarns.
	Filling yarns are frequently novelty yarns.

2. Examine the four samples. Compare the characteristics of each sample to those previously listed and identify the warp and filling yarns in each sample. Mount the sample with the warp yarns placed vertically and the filling yarns placed horizontally.

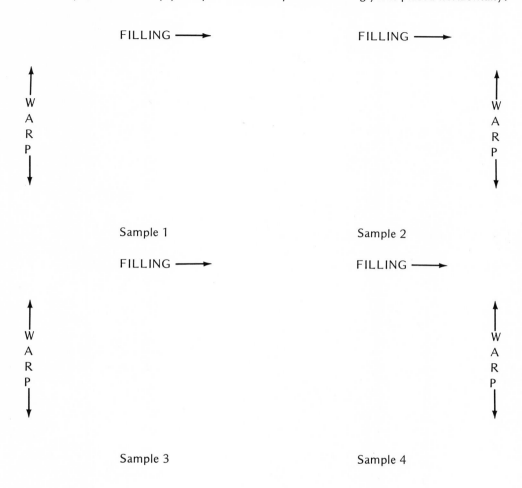

FILLING ⟶   FILLING ⟶

W
A
R
P

Sample 1   Sample 2

FILLING ⟶   FILLING ⟶

W
A
R
P

Sample 3   Sample 4

PART 2: WOVEN FABRICS

Reference Chapter 14, *Understanding Textiles* or assigned readings in text or reference books.

Woven fabrics are constructed by interlacing warp and filling (or weft) yarns at right angles. By varying the points at which yarns interlace, a wide variety of fabric constructions can be made. There are three basic weave structures: the plain weave, the twill weave, and the satin weave. Each of these can be made with several variations. There are also a number of more complex weaves known as fancy weaves that are departures from the basic weaves.

A. Basic Weaves—The Plain Weave

The following pages focus on the construction of the basic weaves, on some of the standard fabrics made from each weave, and the influence of the weave structure on the performance of the fabric. In order to aid in the understanding of the structure of each of these basic weaves, students can construct small samples of each of the basic weaves.

**(1) Weaving Exercise: The Plain Weave

Materials

3" X 3" (8 cm X 8 cm) square of poster board or firm cardboard

plastic or metal|yarn needle at least 3" (8 cm) long

pair of scissors

ruler

1 yard (or about 1 meter) of yarn of one color. Use medium to heavy weight of yarn

1 yard (or about 1 meter) of yarn of another color. Use medium to heavy weight of yarn.

Procedure

1. Diagram the plain weave on the graph paper square provided. Fill in a black square on the graph paper for each point where a warp yarn appears on the right side of the fabric. Leave the square white at each point where a filling yarn appears on the surface of the fabric.

2. The pattern for the plain weave is as follows:
   row 1 (crosswise) Filling crosses over warp #1, under warp #2, over warp #3, under #4, and so on. Leave squares white where the filling crosses the warp (appears on the surface) and darken squares where the filling goes under the warp (the warp appears on the surface.) The diagram for row 1 would be square 1 is white, square 2 is black, square 3 is white, and so on.
   row 2 Filling goes under warp #1, over warp #2, under #3, over #4, and so on. The diagram for row 2 would be square 1 is black, square 2 is white, square 3 is black, and so on.
   row 3 Repeat row 1.
   row 4 Repeat row 2.
   Continue alternating rows 1 and 2 until the graph paper is filled.

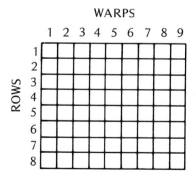

3. Preparation of the loom, the warp, and the weft or filling.

The Loom

1. From the cardboard cut a square 3" X 3" (8 X 8 cm). Mark it off as shown on the following full-scale diagram.

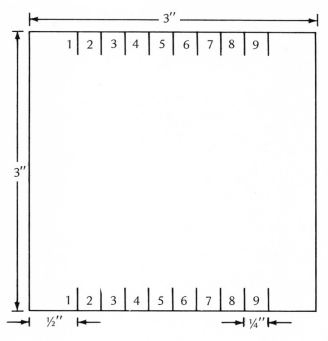

Diagram 3-1.

1. Cut square 3″ X 3″

2. Mark and cut nine slits at the top and bottom of the square, #1 beginning one-half inch from the corner and slit #9 ends one-half inch from opposite the corner. The slits should be at one-fourth inch intervals.

3. Cut slits one-fourth inch deep.

4. Number each slit at the top and the bottom of the loom.

The Warp

1. Fasten the warp yarns to the loom following the diagram, keeping the tension as even as possible.

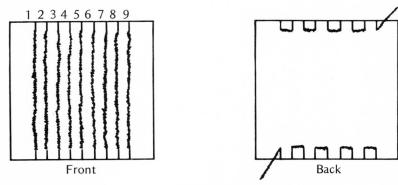

Diagram 3-2.
Preparation of the warp for the plain weave.

The Filling (Weft)

1. Thread filling yarn through a yarn needle. Use a yarn of a color that contrasts with the warp yarn.

Weaving the Plain Weave:

1. Follow the graphed pattern for the plain weave. The light squares indicate that the yarn needle passes over the warp yarn, dark squares indicate that the yarn needle passes under the warp. Continue weaving back and forth across the sample until a sample about two inches (5 cm) in length has been made. After each passage of the yarn, use the needle to push the yarn close to the yarn above it. Mount the completed sample in the space provided.

(3) Examination and Identification of Standard Fabrics in the Plain Weave.

Materials
 set of five or more standard fabrics made in the plain weave, fabric samples to measure not more than 2″ (5 cm) in the warp and 3″ (8 cm) in the filling
 linen tester
 pick needle

1. The instructor will identify the fabric types as they are distributed. Record the name of each sample.

2. Read the definition of each fabric sample in the reference material and record the definition in the space provided beneath the sample mounting.

3. Examine the fabric sample. Look at it first without the linen tester to identify the characteristics described in the definition.

4. Examine the sample with the linen tester to see the construction more closely.

5. These samples will also be used in exercise (4). Mount the samples in the manual after completing exercise (4).

Sample 1
definition

Sample 2
definition

Sample 3
definition

Sample 4
definition

Sample 5
definition

(4) Thread Count

With the use of a linen tester[1] calibrated in inches and fractions of an inch, the number of yarns in one inch of the warp and in one inch of the filling can be counted. When the number of yarns in the warp is the same or almost the same as the number of yarns in the filling, the weave is said to be a *balanced* weave. Balanced weave counts are generally within a range of five yarns more in the warp direction than in the filling direction. Thus, a thread count of 83 in the warp and 79 in the filling could be considered in balance. Thread counts are usually taken at several places in the fabric and are then averaged. Thread counts taken near the selvage are often inaccurate, as yarns in this part of the fabric may be packed more tightly. Thread counts are thus not usually made there.

Thread count is expressed in numerical form: 80 X 64, for example, meaning that there are 80 warp yarns per inch and 64 filling yarns per inch. The number of warp yarns is always written first. When a fabric has a balanced weave, it may also be expressed as 80 square, meaning that there are 80 yarns in the warp and 80 yarns in the filling. This could also be designated as 160 threads per square inch.

Materials and Apparatus

use fabric samples from exercise (3) "Examination and Identification of Standard Fabrics in the Plain Weave"

linen tester

pick needle

Procedure

1. View samples with the warp direction running vertically and the filling direction running horizontally.

2. Place the linen tester over the fabric sample, with the edge of the calibrated section following the filling yarns. Do not move the linen tester while counting the yarns. Complete the weave count for the warp, then count the filling yarns. (Note: Use the pick needle as a pointer to assist in counting, if necessary.) Count the number of warp yarns in one inch, or if the linen tester is smaller than one inch, multiply the number of yarns in one quarter or one half inch to determine how many threads there would be in one inch. In very close or complicated weaves it may be easier to count yarns by unraveling a few yarns along the edge of the fabric in order to expose all of the yarns for counting.

3. Count the number of warp yarns per inch in sample no. 1
... There are_____warp yarns per inch in this sample.

4. Count the number of filling yarns per inch in sample no. 1.
... There are_____filling yarns per inch in sample no. 1.

5. Write the thread count for sample no. 1:____ X_____
... Does this sample have a balanced weave? _____

6. Select any two other samples from the five samples on which to make a thread count. Select one that appears to have a fairly well-balanced weave and one that looks as if it might have a poorly balanced weave. Perform a thread count on each sample.

[1]See Appendix B, II.

Record the results in the space provided:

sample #_____ . Thread count is_____ .

sample #_____ . Thread count is_____ .

7. Mount the samples in the space provided under exercise (3).

B. Basic Weaves—Plain Weave Variations

(1) Examination and Identification of Standard Fabrics in the Basket Weave

Materials and Apparatus

two samples of standard basket weave fabrics measuring not more than 2″ (5 cm)
in the warp by 3″ (8 cm) in the filling
linen tester
pick needle

Procedure

1. The instructor will identify the fabric types as they are distributed. Record the name of each sample.

2. Read the definition of each standard fabric in the reference material, and record in the space provided beneath the sample mounting.

3. Examine the construction of the fabric sample with and without the linen tester.

4. Perform a thread count on one of the samples. Record the thread count under the definition of the sample.

5. Diagram the construction of one of the samples on the graph paper provided. Darken one square of the graph each time a warp yarn appears on the surface of the fabric. Leave squares white when filling yarns appear on the surface. Mount the diagrammed sample beside the graph paper.

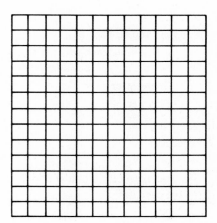

sample
definition

6. Mount the other sample(s) below.

(2) Rib and Cord Variations of the Plain Weave

Ribbed or corded fabrics are created by grouping a number of yarns together before they are woven into the fabric in either direction, or by using yarns that are larger in one direction than in another. When there are enlarged yarns in the filling the resultant fabric is a crosswise rib or cord; a lengthwise rib or cord is formed when the enlarged yarns run in the warp direction.

Materials and Apparatus
   one sample each of a rib or cord fabric, not larger than 2" (5 cm) in the warp and
   3" (8 cm) in the filling
   linen tester
   pick needle

Procedure

1. The instructor will identify the fabric types as they are distributed. Record the name of each sample.

2. Read the definition of the standard fabric in the reference material and record the definition in the space provided beneath the sample mounting.

3. Examine the fabric construction of each sample with and without the linen tester. Determine whether the enlarged yarn in each sample is in the warp or filling direction.

4. Mount samples in the space provided.

Sample 1   Sample 2

Is the rib or cord in the warp   Is the rib or cord in the warp or
or filling direction?   filling direction?

_____   _____

definition: definition:

_____   _____

_____   _____

(3) Effect of Abrasion on Rib or Cord Fabrics

      The balance of a weave is often related to its ability to withstand abrasion. Abra-
sion is the "wearing away of any part of a material by rubbing against another surface."[2]
Rib and cord weave constructions require that some yarns float in a raised position on the
surface of the fabric. As a result, these yarns receive greater exposure to abrasion, whereas in a balanced plain weave, the abrasion is shared more equally by all yarns. For an
illustration of the effect of abrasion on rib or cord weave fabrics as compared with more
balanced plain weave fabrics, the following experiment can be carried out.

**Materials and Apparatus
      fabric samples: one of rib or cord fabric, one of well-balanced plain weave. The
      size of samples required will be determined by the model of abrasion tester being
      used. Retain a control sample of each fabric for purposes of comparison.
      abrasion tester

Procedure

1. Follow the instructions for use of the abrasion tester and abrade test specimens of
   each fabric.

2. Examine the test specimens after abrasion and compare the abraded specimens to
   the control samples.

3. Answer the questions on page 63. Mount the test specimens and control samples in
   the space provided on that page.

[2]1976 ASTM *Annual Book of Standards.* (Philadelphia: American Society for Testing Materials,
1976), part 32, p. 14.

If the laboratory is not equipped with an abrasion tester, the following nontechnical test can be carried out.

**Materials and Apparatus
     two fabric samples 3" (8 cm) square of ribbed or corded fabric
     two fabric samples 3" (8 cm) square of balanced, plain weave fabric
     medium weight sandpaper
     small wood block

Procedure

1. Wrap a piece of sandpaper around the block of wood.

2. Stroke the sandpaper back and forth across the surface of one of the ribbed or corded fabric samples. This is the test specimen. Stroke 10 times in the warp direction, and then 10 times in the filling direction. Try to keep the pressure as uniform as possible.

3. Repeat steps 1 and 2 with a test specimen of balanced, plain weave fabric. Use a fresh piece of sandpaper for each new specimen that is tested.

4. Examine the test specimens. Compare them to the control samples. Describe the effect of abrasion on the appearance of the specimens, and record in the space provided beneath the sample after mounting.

control sample: ribbed or corded
fabric

test specimen: ribbed or corded
fabric

Effect of abrasion on the appearance of the fabric: _____
_____
_____
_____
_____

control sample: balanced plain weave fabric   test specimen: balanced plain weave fabric

Effect of abrasion on the appearance of the fabric: _____
_____
_____

Questions

. . .From this experiment, what conclusion can be drawn about the effect of abrasion on
fabrics constructed with a rib or cord weave as compared with a balanced weave fabric
of the same fiber content? _____
_____
_____
_____

. . .Why is it important to compare fabrics made from the same fibers? _____
_____
_____
_____

C. Basic Weaves—The Twill Weave

The simplest twill weave is created by the filling or weft crossing in a pattern of
over two warp yarns, then under one. In each row, the interlacing with the warp yarn
begins one yarn further on. This progression of interlacing of yarns creates a diagonal
effect in the fabric. The text describes other, more complex patterns of interlacing.

Read the section in the text that deals with twill weaves before constructing the
twill weave sample. Using the same tools as those used in constructing the plain weave
sample, a sample of twill weave can be made.

**Materials and Apparatus

cardboard loom constructed as in (1) Weaving Exercise: The Plain Weave, p. 55.

plastic or metal yarn needle at least 3" (8 cm) long

1 yard (or about 1 meter) of yarn of one color. Use medium to heavy weight.

1 yard (1 meter) of yarn in a contrasting color. Use medium to heavy weight.

Procedure

1. Diagram the twill weave as follows on the graph squares.
   Row 1: Over warp #1 (white square) under warp #2 (black square) over warps #3 & 4 (white squares) under #5 (black), over #6 & 7, under #8, and over #9.
   Row 2: Repeat row 1
   Row 3: Under warp #1, over #2 & 3, under #4, over #5 & 6, over #7, under #8 & 9
   Row 4: Repeat row 3.
   Row 5: Over warps #1 & 2, under #3, over #4 & 5, under #6, over #7 & 8.
   Row 6: Repeat row 5.
   Row 7: Repeat row 1, and go on repeating rows 1 to 6 until the graph paper is filled.

Warps

1 2 3 4 5 6 7 8 9

Rows

1
2
3
4
5
6
7
8
9
10
11
12

2. Prepare the loom as in the following diagram.

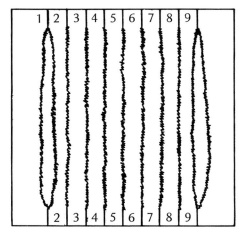

Diagram 3-3.

Preparation of the warp for twill and satin weaves.

(Front side)

3. The slots for warps 1 and 9 each carry two warp yarns. The outermost yarn is used to secure the filling at the end of each passage of the yarn across the fabric. This yarn does not enter into the pattern as diagrammed on the graph. Instead, in every row, regardless of the pattern, the filling yarn must interlace with the outermost warp yarn in the direction opposite to the direction in which the same yarns interlaced in the previous row. (For example, if the filling crossed over the outermost yarn in the first row, it must go under this yarn in the second row, over in the third, under in the fourth, and so on.)

4. Following the diagram, construct a twill weave sample of about two inches in length. Mount the completed sample in the space provided.

(3) Examination and Identification of Standard Fabrics in the Twill Weave

Materials and Apparatus

a set of five or more samples of standard fabrics made in the twill weave, each sample not larger than 2″ (5 cm) in the warp and 3″ (8 cm) in the filling
linen tester

Procedure

1. The instructor will identify the fabric types as they are distributed. Record the name of each sample.

2. Read the definition of the standard fabric in the reference material and record it in the space provided beneath the sample mounting.

3. Examine the fabric sample. Look at it first without the linen tester to identify the characteristics described in the definition.

4. Examine the sample with the linen tester in order to see the construction more closely. Mount the sample.

Sample 1
definition

Sample 2
definition

Sample 3
definition

Sample 4
definition

Sample 5
definition

D. Basic Weaves—The Satin Weave

**(1) Weaving a Sample of Satin Weave Fabric

Satin weave fabrics are made by allowing yarns to float over a number of yarns from the opposite direction. Interlacings are made at intervals such as over four, under one; or over seven, under one; or over eleven, under one. When the warp yarns form the floats, the fabric is referred to as *satin*. When the filling yarns float, the fabric is called *sateen*.

Materials and Apparatus

    1 yard (or about 1 meter) of yarn of one color. Use medium to heavy weight yarn.

    1 yard (or about 1 meter) of yarn of a contrasting color. Use medium to heavy weight yarn.

    cardboard loom constructed as in (1) Weaving Exercise: The Plain Weave, p. 55.

    plastic or metal yarn needle at least 3" (8 cm) long

Procedure

1. Diagram the satin weave on the graph paper as follows:
   Row 1: Over warp #1 (white square), under warps #2–5 (black squares), over #6 (white square), under #7-9 (black squares)
   Row 2: Under warps #1 & 2, over #3, under #4-7, over #8, under #9.
   Row 3: Under warps #1-4, over #5, under #6-9.
   Row 4: Under warp #1, over warp #2, under warps #3-6, over #7, under #8-9.
   Row 5: Under warps #1-3, over #4, under #5-8, over #9
   Row 6: Repeat row one, and so on until the graph paper is filled.

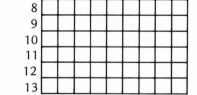

2. Prepare the warp as in the twill weave, Diagram 3-3, p. 64. As in the twill weave, the outermost warps serve to secure the filling yarns and do not enter into the pattern.

3. Following the graph, weave a satin weave sample about two inches in length. Mount the sample in the space provided.

(3) Examination and Identification of Standard Fabrics in the Satin and Sateen Weaves

Materials and Apparatus

    a set of five or more samples of standard fabrics in the satin and sateen weaves, not larger than 2″ (5 cm) in the warp and 3″ (8 cm) in the filling

    linen tester

Procedure

1. The instructor will identify the fabric types as they are distributed. Record the name of each sample.

2. Read the definition of the standard fabric in the reference material and record it in the space provided beneath the sample mounting.

3. Examine the fabric sample. Look at it first without the linen tester to find the characteristics described in the definition.

4. Examine the sample with the linen tester to see the construction more closely. Mount the sample.

Sample 1
definition

Sample 2
definition

Sample 3
definition

Sample 4
definition

Sample 5
definition

E. Fancy Weaves—Jacquard, Dobby and Others

Fabrics may be constructed in a variety of fancy weaves. Samples of standard or characteristic fabrics in the most important of these fancy weaves will be distributed in order to acquaint students with these weaves.

Materials
 set of samples in different fancy weave constructions, each sample not larger than 2" (5 cm) in the warp by 3" (5 cm) in the warp by 3" (8 cm) in the filling
 linen tester

Procedure

1. Read the section in the text concerning each of the fancy weaves.

2. The instructor will identify the fabric types as they are distributed. Record the name of each sample.

3. Examine the sample with and without the linen tester.

4. Mount the swatch in the space provided in the manual. Record the definition of the fabric beneath the sample if it is a standard fabric.

(1) Jacquard Weave

Damask
definition

Brocade
definition

Examine the sample to see the variation of weaves used in the pattern and background areas. From your examination of the sample and the definition of single and double damask, determine whether this sample is a single or double damask.

_____

Look carefully at the sample using the linen tester. Unravel a few filling yarns to determine how many different yarn colors and types of yarns have been used to create the pattern.
No. of colors? _____

No. of yarns? _____
Unravel a few warp yarns to determine how many colors and types of yarns have been used.
No. of colors? _____
No. of yarns _____

Brocatelle
definition

(2) Dobby Weave

Sample 1   Sample 2

Comparing the Jacquard samples to the dobby weave samples, what difference can be
seen in the size of the patterns produced on each loom? _____
_____
_____
_____

F. Other Weaves

(1) Leno Weave

Sample 1   Sample 2

Draw a diagram of the construction of the leno weave as it can be observed under the
linen tester:

(2) Woven Pile Fabrics

corduroy
definition

velveteen
definition

      Unravel enough yarn to release the pile from both the corduroy and velveteen samples. Look at the small pieces of pile and determine whether the pile segment is in the shape of a V or a W. Determine from your text whether the V-shaped pile or the W-shaped pile is more durable, and why. Explain. _____

_____

_____

_____

Unravel a few yarns from the warp and few yarns from the filling of the corduroy and velveteen. Around which set of yarns does the pile wrap? _____

From this determine whether the pile yarn was inserted as warp or as filling.

Is the pile cut or uncut? _____

velvet
definition

terry cloth
definition

Is the velvet pile cut or uncut?

_____

Unravel a few yarns from the warp
and a few yarns from the filling.
Around which set of yarns does
the pile wrap?

_____

From this determine whether the
pile yarn was inserted in the
warp or in the filling.

_____

Is the terry cloth pile cut or uncut?

_____

Is the pile the same or different
on both sides?

_____

If the pile is different, how does one side
differ from the other?_____

_____

When several yarns are pulled down
at the lower edge of the sample, what
yarn length differences can be
observed? _____

_____

Which yarn is longer, the regular
yarn or the pile yarn, Why?

(3) Surface Weaves

Sample 1: name _____

Is the effect yarn used
in the warp or in the filling?

definition

Sample 2: name _____

Is the effect yarn used in the
warp or in the filling?

definition

Sample 3: name_____
Is the effect yarn used
in the warp or in the filling?

definition

(4) Embroidery

Sample 1

Compare embroidered fabrics with surface weave fabrics mounted previously. List some ways in which embroidery differs from the surface weaves.

_____

_____

_____

_____

(5) Multicomponent Fabrics—Interwoven Fabrics

Sample 1: double-faced
fabric made with three sets of
yarns. Examples: double-faced
satin, some blanket fabrics.
Fabric is a single layer throughout.

Sample 2: fabric made with
four sets of yarns, two warps, and
two fillings. Yarns from both
layers move back and forth from
one layer to the other. In some
areas fabrics are totally separated,
in others all four sets of yarns
are interwoven. Examine the
cut edges of fabric for small
pockets where fabric layers
are separate. Matelasse is a
standard fabric in this weave.

Sample 3: Interwoven fabric made
with five sets of yarns, two warp,
two filling, a binder yarn. Take a
pair of scissors and clip away binder
yarn in one corner of the sample.
The two segments of the fabric
can be separated into two distinct
pieces of fabric.

(6) Quilting

thread-stitching sample

thermal stitching sample

By clipping some of the thread, separate one corner to see different layers of fabric. Perform a thread count on the outer, fashion fabric and a thread count on the backing fabric.

outer fabric _____ X _____

backing _____ X _____

separate one corner of the fabric to see the different layers. What fiber property must the three layers have in common in order for this type of stitching to be used?

_____

_____

Thread count outer fabric _____ X _____

Thread count backing _____ X _____

Is it reasonable to expect comparable wear from both the backing fabric and outer fabrics? _____ on the thread-stitched sample? _____
on the thermal-stitched sample? _____
Why? _____

_____

Stretch each of these fabrics on the bias to determine whether the stitches will break under tension. If they break, what performance problems is the consumer likely to encounter with this fabric? _____

_____

_____

_____

_____

(7) Laminated or Bonded Fabrics

Fabric-to-fabric bonding sample possible end uses.

Fabric-to-foam lamination sample possible end uses.

_____

_____

_____

_____

(8) Triaxial Weave Fabrics

The newest type of weave is the triaxial weave. (See *Understanding Textiles*, pp. 215–216). Although specific end uses for the fabric have not yet been determined, the fabric produced has stability in the bias that is superior to conventionally woven fabrics.

PART 3: KNITTED FABRICS

Reference Chapter 15, *Understanding Textiles* or assigned readings in text or reference books.

Knitted fabrics are made by looping together stitches made of a single yarn or set of yarns. In *warp* knits one or more yarns are allotted to each needle on the machine and these yarns follow the vertical or warp direction of the fabric. For *filling* or *weft* knits, one or more yarns are utilized for each crosswise row of stitches, and the yarns move horizontally, or across the filling or weft direction of the fabric.

The rows of stitches that run in a vertical column along the lengthwise direction of the fabric are called *wales*. Crosswise rows of stitches or loops are called *courses*.

*(1) Identification of Wales and Courses in Knit Fabric

Materials

two samples of plain knit fabric 2″ (5 cm) in the warp and 3″ (8 cm) in the filling
linen tester

Procedure

1. Examine the two samples of plain knitted fabric with the linen tester. Look at both sides of each fabric. Determine on which side the wales are more visible and on which side the courses are more visible.

2. Mount one sample so that the side on which the wales are more pronounced is uppermost, and mount the other sample so that the side on which the courses are more visible is uppermost.

wales uppermost   courses uppermost

*(2) Gauge Count

The size of the needles used in knitted fabrics and the spacing of the needles determine the size of the knit stitches and their closeness. The term *gauge* is used to describe the closeness of the knit stitches. Higher gauge fabrics (those with more stitches) are more dense than those of a lower gauge.

A comparison of the gauge of knit fabrics can be made by counting the number of wales and courses in either one inch or one-and-one-half inches of fabric. This count for knits is comparable to the thread count of woven fabrics.

Materials

one sample of plain knit, 2″ (5 cm) in the warp and 3″ (8 cm) in the filling

linen tester

pick needle

Procedure

1. Place the linen tester on the right side of the fabric sample, aligning the edge of the tester along a vertical column of loops. Count the number of vertical stitches in one inch. Record the number in the space provided.

2. Turn the sample to the wrong side where the courses are more visible. Align the tester along a horizontal row of loops. Count the number of stitches in one inch. Record the number in the space provided.

3. Mount the sample in the space provided.

Gauge count:

stitches per inch—wales _____
stitches per inch—courses _____

A. Filling or Weft Knits

Filling or weft knits are made on a number of different knitting machines. These different machines construct knits with varying appearance characteristics that can be distinguished one from the other through examination.

(1) Examination of Samples of Filling Knit Fabrics in the Plain or Jersey Knit

A jersey or plain knit fabric is smooth, the wales highly visible on the right side and the courses more visible on the wrong side. By varying the fibers used in the yarn, the type of yarn, and/or the size or texture of the yarn, a wide variety of fabrics having different appearance and characteristics can be constructed.

Materials and Apparatus

four samples of plain (jersey) knit fabric, 2″ (5 cm) in the warp and 3″ (8 cm) in the filling. Each sample should have different yarns, fibers, gauge, etc.

linen tester

Procedure

1. The instructor will provide information concerning yarn type, fiber content, and so forth for each sample. Record this information in the space provided beneath the sample mounting.

2. Examine the construction of the sample with and without the linen tester. (Examining the sample without the linen tester will provide practice in identifying plain knit fabrics; using the linen tester will enable one to see the construction more clearly.)

3. Mount the samples in the space provided.

Sample 1
Notes:

Sample 2
Notes:

Sample 3
Notes:

Sample 4
Notes:

Questions

. . .Even though each of these fabrics is made with different fibers, yarns, or decorative effects, all show certain similarities of appearance and construction. Identify these similarities and list them.

(2) Examination of High Pile Knitted Fabrics and Knitted Terry and/or Velour

The jersey or plain knit machine is also used to knit high pile, terry, and velour fabrics.

Materials and Apparatus

one sample each of high pile knitted fabric, and knitted terry or velour 2" (5 cm) in the warp by 3" (8 cm) in the filling
linen tester

Procedure

1. Examine each fabric sample with the linen tester.
2. Determine whether the pile or the loop or velour appears on one side or both sides of the fabric.
3. If the pile or loop appears only on one side, is it on the face or on the back?
4. Pull the knitted pile sample apart at the edge. Notice the pile substance. Is it made of yarns or fiber bundles (sliver)?
5. Mount the samples. Label each with any information provided concerning fiber content, etc.

Sample 1
Notes:

Sample 2
Notes:

(3) Examination of Purl Knit Fabrics

The purl knit machine (also called the links-links machine) draws every other course to the opposite side of the fabric. The machine is very versatile, and can construct not only purl knit fabrics but also plain and rib knits. For this reason, purl knit fabrics may be made in complex patterns.

Materials and Apparatus

two samples of purl knit fabric, 2″ (5 cm) in the warp and 3″ (8 cm) in the filling

linen tester

Procedure

1. Examine the samples with and without the linen tester.

2. Mount the samples in the space provided. Label with any information provided concerning fiber content, etc.

Sample 1
Notes:

Sample 2
Notes:

Questions

. . .Describe the appearance of both sides of the sample. _____
_____
_____
_____

. . .What differences can be observed between the plain knit stitch and the purl knit?
_____
_____
_____

(4) Examination of Rib Knit Fabrics

The rib knitting machine constructs fabric by knit and purl alternating on the face and back of the cloth. If stitches alternate in every other stitch, the fabric has a 1 X 1 rib; if every two stitches alternate, the fabric has a 2 X 2 rib; and so on.

Materials and Apparatus

two samples of rib knit fabric, 2" (5 cm) in the warp by 3" (8 cm) in the filling
linen tester
pick needle

Procedure

1. Examine the construction of the sample with and without the linen tester. Using the pick needle, count the number of stitches in the rib. Identify the type of rib in the space provided following the sample mounting.

2. Mount the sample in the space provided.

Sample 1   Sample 2

_____ X _____ rib   _____ X _____ rib

(5) Examination of Double Knit Fabrics

Double knits are made on a rib knitting machine or on an interlock machine. The double knit is a variant of the rib knit. Twice as much yarn is incorporated into a double-knit fabric as into a comparable single-knit fabric.

*Materials and Apparatus

two samples of double knit fabric, each 2" (5 cm) in the warp by 3" (8 cm) in the filling
one sample of single-knit fabric, 2" (5 cm) in the warp and 3" (8 cm) in the filling
linen tester
pencil

Procedure

1. Examine the double knit sample with and without the linen tester. Compare the appearance of the double knit with that of the single knit. List the differences that can be observed in appearance.

2. Place the double knit sample flat against the manual page in the area provided for mounting. Trace around the sample with a pencil. Hold the left side of the sample flat against the paper while pulling on the right side. Mark the point to which the sample stretches.

3. Follow the same procedure with the single knit. Which sample shows greater stretch? _____ Why? _____

4. Mount the samples in the space provided.

single knit sample   double knit sample

double knit sample

(6) Comparison of the Characteristics of Types of Filling Knit Fabrics

Materials and Apparatus

    samples of knits from exercises (1) through (5)
    linen tester

Procedure

1. Examine the samples mounted in exercises (1) through (5). On Chart 3-1, describe the characteristics of each of the types of filling or weft knits. When completed, this chart should provide a comparison of the appearance of these knits that will aid in their identification.

CHART 3-1 COMPARISON OF APPEARANCE OF PLAIN KNIT FABRICS				
	Plain Knit	Purl Knit	Rib Knit	Double Knit
General appearance of the face				
General appearance of the back				

B. Warp Knits

Diagram 3-4 compares the structure of filling and warp knits. With the eye, follow a vertical row of stitches in each diagram (the darker line). Note how each stitch in the filling knit interloops with the stitch directly above it and the stitch directly below it. By contrast, stitches in the warp knit interloop not with the stitches directly above and below, but with stitches in different rows.

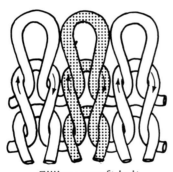 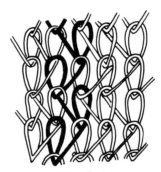

Filling or weft knit   Warp knit

Diagram 3-4.

Comparison of the vertical interlacing of filling and warp knits.

*Materials and Apparatus
    one sample of warp knit, 2″ (5 cm) in the warp by 3″ (8 cm) in the filling
    one sample of plain, filling knit, 2″ (5 cm) in the warp by 3″ (8 cm) in the filling
    linen tester
    pair of scissors
    pencil

Procedure

Experiment 1

1. Examine both samples under the linen tester in order to get an enlarged view of the structure of both fabrics.

2. With a pair of scissors, snip a single yarn somewhere in the center of each fabric. Pull gently on the fabric sample to see if a run will start. Which sample runs? From the reading in the text and your examination of Diagram 3-4, explain why one sample resists running whereas the other does not. _____

_____

_____

_____

_____

*Experiment 2

1. Using the same fabric samples as were used in Experiment 1, place each sample in the space provided for mounting. Trace around each sample with a pencil.

2. Holding the left side of the filling knit sample flat against the page, stretch the right side. Mark the point of extension of the sample. Repeat, using the warp knit. Which fabric sample shows greater stretch? Which type of knit produces a more stable fabric? Why?_____

_____

_____

filling knit sample   warp knit sample

(2) Tricot Warp Knits

Define tricot: _____

_____

Materials and Apparatus

   four samples of tricot fabrics, each 2″ (5 cm) in the warp by 3″ (8 cm) in the filling
   linen tester

Procedure

1. Examine the fabric samples with and without the linen tester.

2. Mount the samples in the space provided in the manual. Record the information provided by the instructor as to fiber content, type of yarn, or pattern. Note the differences in appearance of the samples that is achieved by the use of varying fibers, yarns, patterns, and textures.

Sample 1   Sample 2
Notes   Notes

Sample 3   Sample 4
Notes   Notes

(3) Raschel Warp Knits

Define Raschel knits

Materials and Apparatus

two samples of Raschel knit fabric, 2" (5 cm) in the warp by 3" (8 cm) in the filling

linen tester

Procedure

1. Examine the samples with and without a linen tester.

2. The instructor will provide special information concerning fiber, yarn, or fabric construction. Record this information beneath the sample mounting.

3. Mount the samples.

Sample 1
Notes

Sample 2
Notes

C. Distinguishing Warp and Filling Knits

**Materials and Apparatus

set of samples of warp and filling knits, 2" (5 cm) in the warp by 3" (8 cm) in the filling. Samples will include a variety of different kinds of knits such as rib, tricot, purl, jersey, Raschel, and double knits.

Procedure

1. Be sure the sample is cut along the lower edge exactly on one course.

2. At the lower edge of the sample, unravel a yarn from the knit, pulling it out of the fabric sample slowly and gradually. Observe the way in which the yarn pulls out of the sample. Compare the sample to the following descriptions:
   a. double knits—two yarns will pull from the edge, side-by-side, across the width of the swatch.
   b. weft or filling knits—one yarn will unravel from one side to the other across the width of the fabric.

c. warp knit—many yarns will be released down from the lower edge of the fabric. One yarn cannot be unraveled across the fabric. Pull the yarns down sharply and a shrinking action can be seen to run vertically up the wales.

3. After examining each sample, identify it as either a filling knit, a double knit, or a warp knit. For filling knit samples, determine whether the sample is a plain knit, purl knit, or rib knit.

4. Record the identification on Chart 3-2. Mount each fabric swatch in the space provided.

CHART 3-2 IDENTIFICATION OF WARP AND FILLING KNITS						
	Check One:		If Sample Is a Filling Knit, Check One:			
	Warp Knit	Filling Knit	Plain	Purl	Rib	Double Knit
Sample 1						
Sample 2						
Sample 3						
Sample 4						

D. Performance of Knit Fabrics

(1) Dimensional Stability

The looped construction of knit fabrics often results in a fabric having poor dimensional stability. Consumers sometimes experience difficulty with shrinkage and/or stretching of knits that results in a distortion of the fabric measurements.

Materials and Apparatus

    five 16″ (40 cm) square samples of a variety of knit fabrics including at least one of each of filling, warp, single, and double knits. Samples will be made from a variety of fibers.

    washing machine

    dryer

    basting thread

    sewing needles

    detergent

    dry-cleaning fluid

Procedure

Note: This procedure is time consuming, so the instructor may divide the class into groups, with each group carrying out one part of the procedure. Each group will report its findings to the class. This experiment may also be assigned as a research project for individual students.

1. At the margin of the fabric mark the direction of warp and filling on each sample.

2. Prepare the test samples. Mark a ten inch (25 cm) square and center lines by hand basting with a needle and thread in a color that contrasts with the fabric. Place the markings as indicated in Diagram 3-5. Use short (2″ to 3″ or 5 cm to 8 cm) sections of basting, not a continuous baste marking. Knot each segment securely.

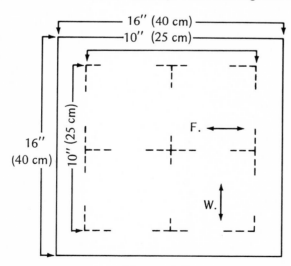

Diagram 3-5.

Preparation of test specimen for test for dimensional change of knit fabrics.

3. Launder or clean all five samples by one or more of the methods assigned by the instructor.

** [2]Method 1: Hand-laundered, dried flat
    1. Launder the samples by hand, using lukewarm water and a mild soap or detergent. Squeeze suds gently through the fabric.
    2. Rinse well and squeeze out excess moisture. Do not wring out or stretch the samples.
    3. Dry flat on a protected tabletop.

*** [2]Method 2: Machine-laundered, line-dried
    1. Launder samples in an automatic or semiautomatic washer. Use a warm-water setting and an all-purpose laundry detergent.
    2. Line dry samples after washing.

**** [2]Method 3: Machine-laundered, dryer-dried
    1. Launder samples in an automatic or semiautomatic washing machine, using warm water and an all-purpose laundry detergent.
    2. Dry samples in an automatic dryer.

*** Method 4: Coin-operated dry cleaning
    1. Clean the samples in a coin-operated dry-cleaning establishment.

** Method 5: Dry cleaned in laboratory
    1. Dry clean in the laboratory following instructions on the dry-cleaning fluid container. (Note: *some dry-cleaning fluids are highly flammable, others require ventilation of the area in which they are used as they produce harmful fumes. Be sure to observe safety precautions appropriate to the dry-cleaning materials being used.*)

4. If the sample requires pressing in order to obtain accurate measurements, press flat with a steam iron set at the appropriate setting for the type of fiber. Press by raising and lowering the iron to the fabric surface. Do not stretch the fabric during pressing.

5. Determine the percentage of shrinkage in the warp as follows:
   a. Measure the warp at each of the three, 10 inch (25 cm) baste markings, converting the fractions into their decimal equivalents.
   b. Add the three measurements and divide by three in order to get the average measurement for the warp.
   c. Using this formula, calculate the percentage of shrinkage.

$$\frac{\text{length of original sample} - \text{length of laundered sample}}{\text{length of original sample}} \times 100 \text{ equals \% shrinkage}$$

If the sample has stretched, rather than shrunk, use this formula:

$$\frac{\text{length of laundered sample} - \text{length of original sample}}{\text{length of original sample}} \times 100 \text{ equals \% of stretch}$$

   d. Repeat the calculations for the filling direction.

6. Prepare a display of samples together with the percentage of shrinkage or stretch that each underwent. Label each sample indicating the cleaning method used. From

----

[2]Drying time will vary.

the display record the data on Chart 3-3. Record stretch as plus values and shrinkage as minus values.

7. Answer the following questions:

. . .Did any samples show consistent patterns of dimensional change no matter what method was used to clean them? Explain.

. . .Did any cleaning method produce consistently good or poor results in maintaining dimensional stability? Explain.

. . .Could any of the results be attributed to fiber content? Explain.

. . .Could any of the results be attributed to the type of knit construction? Explain.

CHART 3-3 DIMENSIONAL STABILITY OF SELECTED KNITS													
Mount small sample here	Type of Knit	Fiber Content	Method 1		Method 2		Method 3		Method 4		Method 5	
			% W	% F	% W	% F	% W	% F	% W	% F	% W	% F

*(2) Snagging

The loop structure of knit fabrics makes them especially susceptible to snagging. A snag occurs when a loop attaches on an object and pulls up from the fabric surfaces.

Materials and Apparatus

three knit samples, 3″ (8 cm) square, each a different type of knit

small piece of unfinished plywood with rough edges, or any other object with a rough surface

crochet hook

Procedure

1. Pull the rough edge of the plywood across the surface of one of the knit samples, first along the length, then across the width.

2. Note whether any snags or loops are pulled up on the surface of the fabric.

3. Describe the results. After completing part 4 of this experiment, mount the samples in the space provided.

Sample 1
Results

Sample 2
Results

Sample 3
Results

Questions

...Does the construction of the knit seem to have any bearing on whether or not the
fabric snags? _____
If so, how is the construction related to the tendency to snag? _____
_____

4. If the snags on some of the knit samples have not broken, try to work the pulled
yarn back into place by pulling the snag to the back of the fabric with the crochet
hook and then gently stretching the fabric. Attempt this with both a tightly knitted
fabric and a more loosely constructed fabric. Which is easier to repair? Why? _____
_____
_____

(3) Pilling

Knits made from loosely twisted yarns may tend to pill. As a result of abrasion
during wear, short fiber ends work their way to the fabric surface and are rubbed into a
small ball that hangs onto the fabric surface.

Standard tests have been developed for determining pilling resistance. ANSI/ASTM
standard test method D1375, reported in the *Annual Book of ASTM Standards Part 33*,
describes one such test. If the laboratory is equipped with either a Brush Pilling Tester or
a Random Pilling Tester, the instructor may demonstrate the tests for pilling on one or
more knit fabrics.

Students can also examine their own wardrobes, by looking at a representative sampling of knit garments. Identify those fabrics that seem to have a tendency to pill. Are these fabrics

1. Usually made from wool, from cotton, or from synthetics? _____

_____

2. Usually made with tight constructions or looser knit constructions? _____

_____

3. Usually made with filament or staple yarns? _____

_____

From this survey, write a brief description of the type of fabric that is most likely to present problems of pilling. _____

_____

_____

PART 4: OTHER FABRIC CONSTRUCTIONS

Reference Chapter 16, *Understanding Textiles* or assigned readings in text or reference books.

A. Nets, Lace, Macrame, and Crochet

Materials and Apparatus
   set of samples characteristic of these fabric constructions, not larger than 2″ (5 cm) in the warp and 3″ (8 cm) in the filling
   linen tester

Procedure

1. The instructor will identify the fabric samples as they are distributed. Record the name of each sample.

2. Examine the sample with and without the linen tester.

3. Mount the swatch in the space provided. Label it with any special information provided by the instructor.

Lace   Net

Macrame   Crochet

Students who are interested in crafts may wish to attempt to construct some or all of these fabric types themselves. The bibliography includes craft books that provide instructions for making these fabrics.

B. Stitch-through Fabric Construction

Materials and Apparatus

sample of fabric constructed by stitch-through process, 2″ (5 cm) in the warp by 3″ (8 cm) in the filling

sample of plain weave fabric, 2″ (5 cm) in the warp by 3″ (8 cm) in the filling

linen tester

Procedure

1. Examine each of the samples using the linen tester. Compare the construction of each of the fabrics. Follow one lengthwise yarn in the structure of each sample. Follow one crosswise yarn.

. . .Describe the visible differences between the structure of the plain weave sample and the structure of the stitch-through sample. _____

_____
_____
_____

. . .Since the warp and filling yarns do not interlace in the stitch-through sample, how is the fabric held together?_____

_____

. . .In what direction do the stitches binding the fabric together move—vertically, horizontally, or diagonally?_____

2. Mount the stitch-through sample in the space provided.

Stitch-through fabric sample

C. Fabric Webs

Fabrics made directly from fibers are usually held together by entangling or bonding and are known as *fabric webs*. Some of these processes, such as felting, are very old. Others represent relatively new developments in textile technology. Many of the products made from fiber webs are disposable; others are more durable.

(1) Felt

*[3] Materials and Apparatus

three samples of felt in light or medium color, each 2″ (5 cm) square, one to be used as a control sample
linen tester

Procedure

1. Examine one of the felt samples under the linen tester. Attempt to see how the fibers are held together.

2. Fray the edge of the sample. Pull on the sample in the warp and filling directions. Is it difficult or easy to break the sample?

3. Launder the second sample by hand, washing it in lukewarm water with a small amount of detergent added. Dry the sample. Compare it to the third, unlaundered sample to determine the following:

    Did the laundered sample display any shrinkage?
    Pull on the sample in the warp and filling directions. Did the sample seem to loose any strength after laundering?

4. From the activities carried out, identify the limitations in use for felt fabrics.

_____

_____

_____

[3] Exclusive of drying time.

5. Mount the samples in the space provided.

(2) Fiber Webs

Materials and Apparatus

      set of samples of fiber webs of different types, each 2″ (5 cm) square

      linen tester

Procedure

1. The instructor will identify the fabric samples as they are distributed. Record the name of each sample.

2. Examine each sample with and without the linen tester.

3. Pull on each of the samples to determine whether they can be pulled apart easily, with some difficulty, or cannot be pulled apart.

**[4]4. The instructor will designate certain samples to be used for the following experiment.
    a. Place the sample on a blank page and trace around the edges.
    b. Wet the sample thoroughly in lukewarm water, then allow it to dry.
    c. Determine whether the sample is the same size after drying as it was before by placing the dry sample over the tracing and comparing.
    d. Determine whether the sample seems to have been affected in any of the following ways by wetting: shrinking, matting, disintegration, or loss of strength.
    e. Mount the samples in the space provided. Write a brief evaluation of the sample as to whether it would be useful in a durable or disposable fabric and why.

5. Mount the remaining samples, labeling them with their trademark and listing some of the common end uses for the product.

[4]Exclusive of drying time.

Sample 1
Useful in durable or disposable goods
Why:

Sample 2
Useful in durable or disposable goods
Why:

Sample 3
End uses:

Sample 4
End uses:

Sample 5 Name
End uses

Sample 6 Name
End uses

UNIT FOUR

Dyeing and Printing

PART 1: DYEING

Reference Chapter 17, *Understanding Textiles* or assigned readings in text or reference books.

*(1) Identifying Fiber, Yarn, and Piece-dyed Fabrics

Color may be added to fibers, to yarns, or to fabrics. Color can also be added to the solution of a man-made fiber before it is spun. Table 4-1 lists the characteristics of fiber-dyed, yarn-dyed, and piece-dyed fabrics that are made from 100 per cent of the same generic fiber.

Table 4-1 CHARACTERISTICS OF FIBER-DYED, YARN-DYED, AND PIECE-DYED FABRICS MADE FROM THE SAME GENERIC FIBER

Fiber-dyed Fabrics	Yarn-dyed Fabrics	Piece-dyed Fabrics
Each yarn consists of different colored or shaded fibers In solid colors, untwisted fibers will be uniform in color with no lighter or darker areas	Warp and filling yarns in pattern area will be different in color Yarns will show no lighter or darker areas where one yarn crosses another Dyes penetrate the yarns well	Fabric will be one solid color When yarns are unraveled they may show lighter and darker areas where they cross other yarns as a result of poor dye penetration

Materials and Apparatus

> 6 fabric samples 2″ (5 cm) in the warp by 3″ (8 cm) in the filling. Each sample made of 100% of the same generic fiber
>
> linen tester
>
> pick needle

Procedure

1. Unravel several yarns from the warp direction and several yarns from the filling direction of one sample.

2. Untwist to examine the fibers.

3. Compare the appearance of the fabric, yarns, and fibers with Table 4-1. Mount a sample of the fabric, and in the space provided beneath the sample identify it as either fiber-, yarn-, or piece-dyed.

4. Repeat this procedure for all samples.

Sample
type of dyeing

Sample
type of dyeing

Sample
type of dyeing

Sample
type of dyeing

Sample
type of dyeing

Sample
type of dyeing

***[1] (2) Differences in Fiber Absorbency

Different fibers absorb dyestuffs depending on the absorption factor of the fiber. Colors penetrate into fibers that absorb well, resulting in a richer, more durable color. This can be observed in the following experiments.

Materials and Apparatus

> sample of white fabric, 2″ (5 cm) in the warp by 3″ (8 cm) in the filling made from a blend or combination of two different generic fibers.
>
> dyestuff
>
> 250 ml beaker
>
> glass stirring rod

[1] Depending upon the specific instructions for the dye that is used.

hot plate or Bunsen burner

tongs

Procedure

1. The instructor will provide the names of the two generic fibers in the sample. Write these names in the space provided beneath the mounted sample.

2. Remove any starch, oils, or waxy finishes from the fabric by immersing the sample in hot water for 15 minutes. This can be done while the dyebath is being prepared.

3. Prepare the dyebath according to the directions on the package of dye, or, if the dyebath has been prepared by the instructor, follow the directions for its use given by the instructor.

4. Place the sample in the dyebath and proceed according to the directions provided. If the dyestuff requires it, heat the dyebath for the required period of time. Rinse well, then dry the sample.

5. When the sample is dry, examine the fabric. Answer the questions that follow, then mount the sample in the space provided.

Questions

. . . Did the entire sample absorb the dye evenly? _____

. . . If not, how is the dye distributed?

. . . Are the lighter colored fibers or yarns in the sample made from the generic fiber that is less absorbent or the one that is more absorbent? Explain.

. . . From your knowledge of the relative absorbency of these two generic fibers, determine the identity of the generic fiber that dyed to the lighter shade._____ To the darker shade. _____

Fiber content   Dyed sample

____ % ____

____ % ____

(3) Cross-dyeing and Union Dyeing

When a blended fabric is dyed, special care must be taken to find dyes that will color each of the different generic fibers to the same shade if that is the desired effect. (In the textile industry this is called *union dyeing*.) The principle of using specific dyes for specific fibers can also be used to produce a *cross-dyed fabric*, that is, a fabric in which the yarns of one fiber absorb a dyestuff of one color and the yarns of another fiber absorb a different dyestuff of another color. These dyes that are specific to a particular fiber can be placed in the same dyebath, and one immersion in the dyebath will produce a multicolored fabric.

Special dye-staining products have been prepared for use in textile identification that utilize this principle. These prepared stains are mixtures of several dye classes and colors, each specific to a particular fiber or class of fibers. The following experiment demonstrates the use of one of these stains.

Materials and Apparatus
1" (3 cm) square samples, one each of cotton, wool, and nylon in white or light colors
Bunsen burner and ring stand or hot plate
250 ml graduated cylinder
stirring rod
T.I.S. Identification Stain #1
distilled water
laboratory thermometer
250 ml beaker

Procedure

1. With an indelible laundry marking pen, indicate the fiber content (c-cotton, w-wool, ny-nylon) on each sample.

2. To remove any starch, wax, or oils present in the samples that would interfere with dyeing, immerse the samples in warm or hot water for 15 minutes. This can be done while the dyebath is being prepared.

3. Prepare a solution of dye. Use 1 gram of T.I.S. stain #1 for each 100 ml of water. (100 ml of stain solution will be adequate for this experiment.)

4. Place the stain solution in a 250 ml beaker and bring the solution to a boil. Add the fabric samples to the beaker. Maintain the temperature and boil for five minutes.

5. Remove the samples. Rinse thoroughly in water at a temperature of 120°F (or 55°C).

6. After the samples are dry, compare the color of the samples to see the differences in colors that one dyebath produced. Mount the samples, labeling each with its generic fiber content.

Sample
fiber content

Sample
fiber content

Sample
fiber content

PART 2: COLORFASTNESS

Reference Chapter 17, pp. 259–260, *Understanding Textiles*; Chapter 23, pp. 362–365, *Understanding Textiles*; or assigned readings in text or reference books.

Some dyestuffs have better colorfastness than others. The same dyestuff may also differ in colorfastness to different conditions. The following tests can be used to determine the colorfastness of fabrics to some of the more common conditions to which fabrics may be exposed. Many of the tests outlined in the following pages can be carried out with little or no specialized equipment. Other standard tests for the evaluation of colorfastness have been established by technical organizations. These tests will be cited, and in those laboratories that have the required equipment the instructor may demonstrate or ask students to carry out these tests following the instructor's directions. All of the following tests should be carried out on samples from the same fabric so that a comparison can be made of colorfastness of one fabric to different conditions.

(1) Colorfastness to Light—Technical Tests

A variety of technical tests for evaluating colorfastness to light are reported in the AATCC *Technical Manual* and in the ASTM *Annual Book of Standards.* The numbers of these tests are AATCC Test Method 16-1974-Colorfastness to Light: General Method, AATCC Test Method 16A-1974-Colorfastness to Light: Carbon-Arc Lamp, Continuous Light, AATCC Test Method 16B-1974-Colorfastness to Light: Sunlight, AATCC Test Method 16C-1974-Colorfastness to Light: Daylight.

If the laboratory has a Fade-Ometer or a carbon-arc lamp fading apparatus, one or more of these tests can be performed. These machines have two advantages over simply exposing samples to daylight or sunlight. They provide accurate control of the quantity of light to which the samples are exposed, whereas the quantity of light provided by the sun will vary depending on the weather, time of year, and direction of exposure or light conditions in the room. Furthermore, the intensity of the light in the apparatus makes possible the completion of testing in a relatively short time. If these tests are performed, fabric samples can be mounted in the space provided at the end of Appendix C. On the same page, describe the test(s) performed, record any data produced, and report the results. Mount both the control sample and the test samples.

*[2] (2) Colorfastness to Light—Nontechnical Test

The following test will provide a general indication of the colorfastness of fabrics to sunlight. This test must be carried out over a period of time and could also be done at home or in a dormitory room.

Materials and Apparatus

two samples of the same fabric for testing, each measuring 2″ (5 cm) in the warp by 4″ (10 cm) in the filling
masking tape

Procedure

1. Tape one test specimen of each fabric to the inside of a window, placing the right side of the fabric toward the glass. If possible, use a window with a southern exposure and one that receives full sun for the entire day.

2. Put the second or control sample away, out of contact with light.

3. Allow for a total of about 40 hours of exposure to sunlight on the mounted specimen, inspecting as follows: Remove the specimen from the window at the end

[2]For preparing the samples.

of 20 hours of exposure and compare to the control sample that was not exposed to the sunlight. Record any color change on the chart. Continue to expose the test specimen for another 20 hours. Evaluate again by comparing it to the control sample that was not exposed.

4. Mount the samples and record the results of the testing on the chart.

Test Specimen   Control Sample

CHART 4-1	Twenty Hours	Forty Hours
Color change	exposed sample	exposed sample
no visible color change		
slight color change		
marked color change		

(3) Colorfastness to Crocking

Some fabrics lose color through crocking or rubbing against another fabric. Some fabrics crock when dry, some do so when both dry and wet.

Technical Test with a Crockmeter

If the laboratory is equipped with a Crockmeter, which is a device for testing crocking, the instructor may demonstrate its use or ask students to carry out a crocking test on the Crockmeter. Follow the instructions provided, then mount the tested samples in the space provided, and answer the questions that follow.

Nontechnical Test of Crocking

*Materials

    2 samples of each colored fabric to be tested, each 4" (10 cm) square

    2 samples of clean white fabric, 2" (5 cm) square

Procedure: dry crocking

1. Place a specimen of the fabric to be tested on a flat surface.

2. Fold a clean, dry, white cotton fabric over the forefinger.

3. Firmly rub *back and forth* across the test specimen 10 times for a total of 20 strokes.

4. Examine the white fabric to determine whether any color has rubbed off.

5. If the laboratory has a Gray Scale for Staining, the degree of color transference can be rated following the directions provided by the instructor.

6. Mount a small sample of each of the tested fabrics in the space provided. Mount the white fabric used for the test beside the samples of tested fabric.

Procedure: Wet crocking

1. Thoroughly wet the second sample of white fabric and squeeze out surplus water until the cloth is damp.

2. Rub the dampened white fabric back and forth across the second specimen of the test fabric 10 times for a total of 20 strokes.

3. Examine the white fabric to see whether any color has rubbed off.

4. Rate the degree of color transference, using the Gray Scale for Staining if available.
    Note: Where this device is not used, rate staining as
        1. no crocking
        2. slight crocking
        3. considerable crocking

Dry crocking		Wet crocking	
Fabric Tested	White Cloth	Fabric Tested	White Cloth

Rating _____   Rating _____   Rating _____   Rating _____

Questions

... Did the fabric crock either dry or wet? _____

... What consumer problems could be produced by a fabric that is subject to dry crocking?

... What consumer problems could be produced by a fabric that is subject to wet crocking?

(4) Colorfastness to Laundering

Technical Tests

AATCC Test Method 61-1972 tests "Colorfastness to Washing, Domestic; and Laundering, Commercial." This accelerated test is carried out in a Launder-Ometer or similar apparatus. If the laboratory has a Launder-Ometer, the instructor may ask students to carry out a test of colorfastness to laundering in this machine. Mount tested samples in the space provided at the back of the manual.

**[3]*Nontechnical Tests*

For those laboratories having no testing equipment, the following test can be used to evaluate colorfastness.

Materials and Apparatus
> two identical samples of fabric to be tested, 4" (10 cm) square
> sample of Multifiber Fabric
> pint jar with a screw top
> detergent or soap powder
> clear glass tumbler or beaker
> 1 cup (about 250 milliliters) of water

Procedure

1. Put one 4 inch (10 cm) square sample aside to be used as a control sample.

2. Staple the Multifiber Fabric to the other fabric sample. This will be the test specimen.

3. Fill the pint jar with one cup (250 milliliters) of water of the correct temperature for this fabric. (See Table of Laundry Procedures: Appendix B, p. 157)

[3]Does not include drying time.

4. Place one half teaspoon of detergent or soap in the jar. Cover the jar and shake it to mix the water and detergent. Place the test specimen in the jar and cover the jar tightly. Shake the jar briskly for one minute. Allow it to stand for five minutes, then shake it again for one minute.

5. Pour the used wash water into the clear glass tumbler or beaker. Look to see if any color has bled into the water. Samples may lose some color without undergoing noticeable color loss themselves. Record this information in the space provided.

6. With the Multifiber Fabric still attached, rinse the sample well, and then dry it with the test specimen on top of the Multifiber Fabric. When both the Multifiber Fabric sample and the test specimen are dry, compare the test specimen to the control sample. If the laboratory has a Gray Scale for Color Change, rate the color change, if any, with this scale. Record the data called for in the questions that follow the mounted samples.

7. Examine the Multifiber Fabric sample to determine whether any of the fibers on this sample have changed in color. If it is available, use the Gray Scale for Staining to rate the staining of the Multifiber Fabric sample. Record the data in the space provided.

8. Mount samples of control fabric, test specimen, and Multifiber Fabric sample in the space provided.

Control Sample   Test Specimen and Multifiber Sample

Questions:

. . . Did the wash water show any color change? _____ If so, was this change slight or quite pronounced? _____

. . . Did the test sample show any observable color change when it was compared to the control sample? _____
Rating on the Gray Scale for Color Change:

. . . Did the Multifiber Fabric sample show any staining? _____

If so, which fiber(s) were stained, and to what extent?

Rating of the Gray Scale for Staining:

... As a result of this test, are there any special care procedures that would be required in laundering this fabric?

(5) Colorfastness to Dry Cleaning

Technical Tests

AATCC Test Method 132-1973, "Colorfastness to Dry Cleaning," requires a Launder-Ometer. If the equipment is available, this test can be used to evaluate the colorfastness of fabrics to dry cleaning. Samples can be mounted at the back of the manual.

*Nontechnical Test

For laboratories that do not have this equipment, the following procedure can be used to evaluate the colorfastness of fabrics to dry cleaning.

Materials and Apparatus

two identical samples of colored fabric, each 4" (10 cm) square

pint jar

small tongs

dry-cleaning fluid (*Note: Observe Caution in Using Dry-Cleaning Solvents; Some are flammable and others may produce noxious fumes. Use only under supervision and follow directions very carefully.*)

Procedure

1. Put one four inch (10 cm) square sample aside to be used as a control sample. The other fabric sample will be the test specimen.

2. Fill the pint jar half full with the dry-cleaning fluid.

3. Immerse the test specimen in dry-cleaning fluid for five minutes.

4. With the tongs, remove the specimen from the fluid. Examine the fluid to determine whether there has been any color change.

5. Dry the specimen on paper towels. Compare it to the control sample. Determine whether any color change has taken place. The specimen can be rated on the Gray Scale for Color Change.

6. Mount the test specimen and the control sample in the space provided. Answer the questions.

Control Sample   Test Specimen

Questions

. . . Did the test specimen show any observable color change when it was compared to
the control sample?
What was the rating on the Gray Scale for Color Change?

(6) Colorfastness to Bleaching with Chlorine

Technical Tests

AATCC Test Method 3-1972, "Colorfastness to Bleaching with Chlorine" requires
the use of a Launder-Ometer. If the equipment is available, this test can be used to test
the colorfastness of fabrics to bleaching with chlorine.

***[4]*Nontechnical Test*

For those laboratories without this equipment, the following procedure can be
used to test colorfastness to bleaching with chlorine bleach.

Materials and Apparatus
two identical fabric samples, 4" (10 cm) square
hot plate or Bunsen burner and ring stand
200 ml beaker
laboratory thermometer
small tongs
liquid chlorine bleach
water

Procedure

1. Put one four inch (10 cm) square sample aside to be used as a control sample. The
    other fabric sample will be used as the test specimen.

2. Dilute 25 ml of liquid chlorine bleach with 125 ml of water. Using the hot plate or
    Bunsen burner heat the water to a temperature of 105–110°F or 40–45°C.

3. Place the test specimen in the water. Allow the specimen to remain in the water for
    30 minutes, maintaining the heated temperature throughout the test time. After 30
    minutes, remove the specimen using tongs.

[4]Does not include drying time.

4. Rinse the specimen thoroughly in tap water and dry. Compare the color of the bleached specimen to the unbleached control sample.

5. If a Gray Scale for Color Change is available, rate the color change by the scale.

6. Mount the control sample and the test specimen in the space provided. Answer the questions.

Control Sample   Test Specimen

Questions

. . . Did the test specimen show any observable color change when it was compared to the control sample? _____

. . . What was the rating on the Gray Scale for Color Change? _____

. . . Review the results of all of the tests for colorfastness that were carried out on this fabric. How would you evaluate the overall colorfastness of the fabric? Explain

_____
_____
_____
_____
_____
_____
_____
_____

PART 3: PRINTING

Reference Chapter 18, *Understanding Textiles* or assigned readings in text or reference books.

One of the simplest techniques for direct printing on a fabric is by block printing. Relatively little fabric is produced commercially by this method, but it is a popular craft technique used for decorating textiles. Students who are interested in experimenting with block printing can find directions in the craft books listed in the bibliography in Appendix A.

Resist printed designs can also be achieved by treating some parts of the fabric with substances that prevent dye penetration. When the fabric is immersed in the dyebath, the areas that are covered will not receive the dye. Two popular craft techniques for coloring fabrics utilize this principle. They are *batik* and tie-and-dye. Books containing instructions for these crafts can also be found in the bibliography.

(1) Examination of a Variety of Printed Fabrics

Materials and Apparatus

    samples of printed fabrics, 2″ (5 cm) in the warp by 3″ (8 cm) in the filling
    linen tester

Procedure

1. The instructor will identify the printed fabric samples and provide any other relevant information concerning each sample.

2. Examine the fabric sample with and without the linen tester.

3. Mount the sample in the manual and answer questions.

Roller print
How many rollers were used to make this print?

Warp print
What are the design characteristics of warp prints?

Blotch print
How can a blotch print be distinguished from a roller print?

Discharge print
What design limitation would this type of print have?

Flock print
What feature identifies a flocked print?

Heat transfer print
Why is heat transfer printing used extensively on knits?

Can heat transfer printing be used successfully on fabrics made from all fibers? Why?

UNIT FIVE

Finishes

References Chapter 19, *Understanding Textiles* or assigned readings in text or reference books.

PART 1: CLASSIFICATION OF FINISHES

Finishes are often classified as temporary and/or renewable, durable, or permanent. Temporary or renewable finishes are those that are removed after one or more launderings or dry cleanings. Durable finishes are those that can be expected to function during a reasonable life for the end product, and permanent finishes are those that will last for the lifetime of the fabric.

Finishes that add body or stiffness to fabrics can be used to demonstrate the difference between a permanent and a temporary finish.

**[1] Materials and Apparatus

    two 2″ (5 cm) square samples of sheer fabric lightly sized with household starch
    two 2″ (5 cm) square samples of permanent-finished organdy fabric
    pint jar with a lid
    detergent

Procedure

1. Put one sample of sized fabric and one sample of organdy fabric aside for the control samples. The other samples will be used as the test specimens.

2. Fill the pint jar with warm water. Dissolve one half teaspoon of detergent in the jar. Agitate the jar to dissolve the detergent.

---

[1] Exclusive of drying time.

3. Place the test specimens in the jar with the lid fastened securely. Shake the jar vigorously for one minute. Allow the jar to stand for five minutes, then shake again for one minute.

4. Pour out the water. Rinse the specimens thoroughly in clear, warm water and dry.

5. When dry, compare the specimens with the control samples.

6. Mount the samples in the space provided. Enter the evaluation of the test specimens beneath the mounted samples.

Starched fabric: Starched fabric: Organdy: Organdy:
control   test specimen   control   test specimen

Condition of test specimen as   Condition of test specimen as
compared to control sample is   compared to control sample is
_____   _____

Questions

. . . Which of the samples had the temporary finish and which had the permanent finish? Can the sample with the temporary finish have the original finish replaced?

If so, how? _____

_____

_____

_____

_____

PART 2: FINISHES AFFECTING APPEARANCE

Some finishes affect the appearance of the fabric. Many of these finishes can be identified merely by observation. A set of samples will be provided for identification and study purposes.

Materials and Apparatus
     set of samples of fabrics with different finishes each measuring 2″ (5 cm) in the warp by 3″ (8 cm) in the filling
     linen tester

Procedure

1. Read the section in the text on finishes that affect the appearance of fabrics.

2. Match each sample from the set of samples to the description that most accurately characterizes the sample. Mount the sample in the appropriate place.

Glazed fabric is fabric with a highly glazed or polished surface. These fabrics have a high shine on the surface. Examination with a linen tester shows that the glazed fabrics are made from staple yarns.

Cire fabrics have a high surface polish, sometimes called "the wet look." Most cires are made from thermoplastic fibers, and under the linen tester the yarns can be seen to have fused slightly. Cire fabrics are made from filament yarns.

Embossed design is design created by pressing a pattern onto the fabric. Designs are often three dimensional.

Moire fabrics have a watered appearance on the fashion side of the fabric, sometimes called a "grain of wood" pattern. Moire finishes are applied to ribbed fabrics.

Napped fabric is fabric in which loose fiber ends are brushed up on the surface of the fabric. Napped fabrics can be distinguished from flocked fabrics by unraveling a yarn and examining it under a linen tester. Since the fibers in napped fabric are an integral part of the yarn, the fibers will project from the yarn surface.

In flocked fabric (pile effect) a nap or pile effect is created by holding short fibers onto the surface of a base with adhesives or a thermoplastic component. Flocked fabrics can be distinguished from napped fabrics by unraveling a yarn and examining the yarn under a linen tester. The yarn is smooth surfaced; the flock is a separate part.

Burnt-out design—created by dissolving out some areas of the fabric. Fabrics are woven from the yarns of two fibers, one yarn being soluble in a particular chemical. The chemical is imprinted in a design on designated parts of the fabric; it dissolves out the soluble fiber leaving some sheer and some heavier areas.

Acid print—creation of transparent areas in the fabric by printing on cotton materials with acids.

118

Plisse—puckered effect created on cotton by treating some areas of the fabric with sodium hydroxide. Treated areas shrink, causing other areas to pucker or bubble up between the shrunken areas. Plisse should not be confused with seersucker. Similar effects are created on fabrics made from other fibers, using chemicals that cause those fibers to shrink (example: nylon treated with phenol.)

Seersucker is achieved in the weaving, not by finishing. Puckers in seersucker are created by holding the warp yarns at differing tensions during weaving giving a permanent blister. Seersucker cannot be stretched flat as can the plisse.

Place the plisse and seersucker samples side-by-side. Stretch each sample. The seersucker cannot be stretched flat; the plisse sample can be stretched flat. Mount the samples.

PART 3: FINISHES AFFECTING PERFORMANCE OF TEXTILES

Reference Chapter 20, *Understanding Textiles* or assigned chapters in text or reference books.

Many different finishes are given to fabrics to alter their performance characteristics. For the most part these finishes cannot be detected in the appearance of the fabric, as the purpose of adding the finish is to improve some aspect of performance in use. A variety of textile tests have been developed to evaluate the effectiveness of these finishes. Most of these tests require specialized testing equipment and controlled conditions. The following few tests have been adapted for use in the classroom or laboratory and serve to illustrate the ways in which these finishes affect the behavior of fabrics. Where the specialized equipment required for technical testing is available, the instructor may demonstrate or ask students to perform a few of the technical tests cited. Students may find it useful to read through the testing procedures in the technical manuals in order to acquaint themselves with some of these tests and the way they are reported.

***[2] (1) Evaluation of Dimensional Change of Woven Fabrics When Laundered

Some fabrics will display shrinkage after laundering. Special finishes may be given to fabrics to assure that they will retain their original dimensions. Tests for dimensional change of woven fabrics can be used to evaluate the effectiveness of such a finish, or to compare two fabrics, one of which has been given such a finish and one of which has not. The same tests can be used for a general evaluation of the dimensional stability of fabrics.

[2]Exclusive of drying time.

Technical Tests

Both the ASTM and the AATCC publications contain test procedures for evaluating dimensional stability. These tests are ASTM Test D 1905-73 Part 33 and AATCC Test Method 96-1972.

Nontechnical Test

Materials and Apparatus

two fabric specimens, 16″ (40 cm) square, one with and one without a shrink resistant finish

washing machine

flat drying surface

hand steam iron

indelible pen

ruler with 1/16th inch or millimeter divisions

detergent

Procedure

1. Prepare two fabric specimens to be tested as follows: Mark off a 10 inch (or 25 cm) square and center lines in indelible ink within the 16 inch (40 cm) sample as shown in Diagram 5-1. Mark the warp and the filling clearly in indelible ink. Be sure that the markings follow the lengthwise and crosswise grain of the fabric exactly.

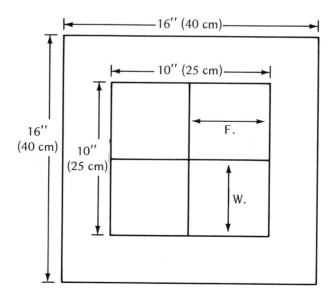

F = filling
W = warp

Diagram 5-1.

Preparation of test specimen for test for dimensional change of a laundered woven fabric.

(Note: if the laboratory does not have laundry equipment, students can launder samples at home, in the dormitory, or in a laundromat with a regular load of wash. Follow the same procedures.)

2. Fill the washer with water of the appropriate temperature for this fabric.

3. Add the amount of detergent recommended for this type of washing machine.

4. Select the correct washing time for this fabric (See chart in Appendix B, p. 000 for water temperature, washing time, and agitation and spin speeds appropriate for different types of fabric.)

5. Allow the fabric to be washed for the full cycle of the washer. Remove the sample from the washer when the cycle is complete. If the washer is a semiautomatic and samples are removed from the rinse water without spin drying, squeeze the sample dry. Do not wring

6. Dry the sample on a protected, flat surface.

7. If the sample requires pressing in order to obtain accurate measurements, press flat with a steam iron at the appropriate setting for the fabric. Press by raising and lowering the iron to the fabric surface. Do not stretch the fabric during pressing.

8. Determine the percentage of shrinkage as follows.
   a. Measure the warp at each of the three, 10 inch (25 cm) markings, converting any fractions into decimal equivalents.
   b. Add the three measurements and divide by 3 to get the average measurement for the warp.
   c. To calculate the percentage of dimensional change use this formula:

$$\frac{\text{length of original sample} - \text{length of laundered sample}}{\text{length of original sample}} \times 100$$

   d. Repeat the same procedure for the filling, measuring the sample at the filling markings.

9. Mount the test specimens in the space provided in Appendix C for mounting large samples. Fill in the percentage of shrinkage for the warp and the percentage of shrinkage for the filling of each sample in the space provided.

CHART 5-1 PERCENTAGE OF WARP AND FILLING SHRINKAGE	
Percentage of Shrinkage in Warp	Percentage of Shrinkage in Filling
Sample with shrink-resistant finish	
Sample without shrink-resistant finish	

Questions

... If the sample without the shrink-resistant finish were made into a garment with a 25-inch waistband cut in the filling direction, how large would that wastiband be after the fabric was laundered?

... If the sample without the shrink-resistant finish were made into a skirt that measured 20 inches in the length or warp, how much would the skirt shrink in that direction after one laundering?

If large fabric samples of more than 10 inches are not available for testing, small samples can be evaluated for dimensional change by measuring the sample, washing it by hand, and then remeasuring it after laundering. The exactness of data cannot be achieved, but a general index of performance can be noted. Fabrics with a tendency to ravel may need to be overcast to prevent the loss of dimensions due to raveling. Calculate the percentage of shrinkage using the formula given in paragraph 8c.

*(2) Absorbency

Some finishes increase the absorbency of fabrics. Other finishes though not intended to increase or decrease absorbency *per se* may nevertheless have this effect. Fabrics that have had soil-resistant finishes may resist wetting in order to prevent soiling or staining. Other finishes, such as soil-releasing finishes or finishes that decrease static electricity buildup, increase absorbency. A simple test for absorbency of fabric follows.

Materials and Apparatus
two fabric specimens, [3]8" (20 cm) square one with a soil-resistant finish, one without a soil-resistant finish
6" embroidery hoop
eyedropper
stopwatch

Procedure

1. Work with an assistant. Place one fabric sample on the hoop, being careful to mount the specimen so that the fabric is free from wrinkles.

2. Place the hoop on a flat surface. One person should hold the eyedropper three-eighths inch above and perpendicular to the specimen and allow one drop of water to fall on the specimen.

3. When the water drop falls on the fabric specimen, the second person should start the stopwatch. Using the stopwatch, record the length of time required for the drop of water to be absorbed by the specimen. The water is absorbed at the precise time when the drop can no longer be seen on the surface of the specimen. Record the time.

4. Repeat twice more, each time dropping the water in a different area of the fabric specimen. Average the wetting time for this fabric and record the average. Record the data on Chart 5-2. Mount a small sample of the test specimen on the chart.

5. Repeat steps 1 to 4 for the second fabric specimen. Compare the results.

[3]When testing fabrics without water-repellent finishes, be sure to launder and dry samples before testing. Unlaundered samples may contain waxes and other finishing materials that will confer some water resistance to the fabric that it will not have after laundering.

CHART 5-2 ABSORBENCY OF SELECTED FABRIC SAMPLES	Wetting Time			
	First Test	Second Test	Third Test	Average
Sample #1				
Sample #2				

good—less than 5 seconds wetting time
poor—more than 5 seconds wetting time

Sample 1   Sample 2

Finish: Finish:
_____   _____

This test can be repeated comparing the absorbency of fabrics having durable press, water-repellent or antistatic or soil-releasing finishes.

**(3) Water Repellency

Fabrics may be given special finishes to improve their ability to repel water. Rainwear is frequently given such finishes. A distinction should be made between *waterproof* finishes and *water-repellent* finishes. A waterproof fabric allows no water to penetrate from the surface to the underside of the fabric. A water-repellent fabric resists penetration by water but is not completely waterproof. The term *water resistant* does not apply to a specific finish, but is a general term "denoting the ability of a fabric to resist wetting and penetration of water."[4] Several tests have been developed that are used to predict the water resistance of fabrics.

Materials and Apparatus

spray tester (made from a ring stand, spray nozzle, and 6″ funnel)[5]
two test specimens 8″ (20 cm) square one with a water-repellent finish, one without
200 ml beaker
250 ml distilled water 80°F or 27°C
stopwatch
6″ (15 cm) embroidery hoop
AATCC Standard Spray Test Rating Chart

Procedure

1. Fasten a test specimen to the hoop so that it is free of wrinkles.

[4]1976 ASTM *Book of Standards*, Part 33, p. 481.

[5]If the laboratory does not have a spray tester, see instructions in AATCC *Technical Manual*, Test Method 22-1974 for its construction.

2. Place the hoop at the base of the stand, at a 45° angle to the stand. The center of the hoop should be placed directly below the nozzle. (See Diagram 5-2.)

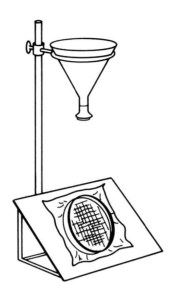

Diagram 5-2.

Apparatus with hoop and specimen in place for spray test.

3. Fill the beaker with 250 ml of water and pour the water into the funnel. The water will spray onto the specimen from the nozzle. This will require about 25 to 30 seconds.

4. Holding the hoop at a 45° angle, sharply tap one edge against a solid object in order to remove any unabsorbed water.

5. Compare the tested specimen to the Standard Spray Test Rating Chart. If no copy of the chart is available, samples can be examined to determine which of the following descriptions they match most closely:
   A. No wetting of the surface of the fabric turned toward the nozzle.
   B. Slight wetting of the surface toward the nozzle.
   C. Wetting of the surface toward the nozzle at spray points.
   D. Partial wetting of the surface toward the nozzle.
   E. Complete wetting of the surface toward the nozzle.
   F. Complete wetting of the surface toward the nozzle and of the underside of the fabric.
   A rating of A indicates good water repellency. A rating of F indicates lack of water repellency.

6. Mount a small sample of the test specimen in the space provided. Fill in the information concerning fiber content and finishes and record the rating.

7. Repeat the test with the other test specimen.

CHART 1-3 WATER REPELLENCY OF SELECTED FABRIC SAMPLES			
Sample	Fiber Content	Finished or Not Finished	Rating

The technical testing procedure on which the preceding test was modeled (AATCC Test Method 22-1974) states that this test is *not* intended to predict the probable rain penetration resistance of fabrics. AATCC Test method 42-1974 will predict rain penetration resistance of fabrics. Read or perform the test and explain why Test Method 42-1974 is said to predict the probable rain penetration resistance of fabrics.

_____

_____

_____

_____

_____

_____

**(4) Fire-Retardant Finishes

Testing of fabrics with fire-retardant finishes is mandated by the Flammable Fabrics Act. The apparatus used and the conditions under which testing is to be done are rigorously controlled in these tests. One of the better known of the many tests for textile flammability is the test reported either as ANSI/ASTM D-1230- Standard Test Method for Flammability of Clothing Textiles, or the one listed in the *AATCC Manual* as Test Method 33-1962. If equipment is available for this test, it can be demonstrated by, or performed under, the supervision of the instructor.

The following simple experiments do not equal these technical tests, but are intended to make some general comparisons between fabrics that have had special flame-retardant finishes or are inherently flame retardant and those that have had no special treatment.

Materials and Apparatus

five samples of each fabric to be tested, each specimen 8″ (20 cm) in the warp by 2″ (5 cm) in the filling

apparatus for burning (See Diagram 5-3 and instructions for constructing this device)

candle or Bunsen burner

stopwatch

Construction of Testing Apparatus

An apparatus for burning tests can be devised from the following materials:

2″ (5 cm) (or larger) metal spring clip

a flat metal sheet at least 12″ long and 8″ wide (30 cm by 20 cm). (A cookie sheet without sides can be used.)

a device for holding the metal sheet at about a 45° angle (An easel or plate holder can be used.)

Clip the spring clip at the top of the metal sheet.

Fasten the specimen to be tested as shown in Diagram 5-3.

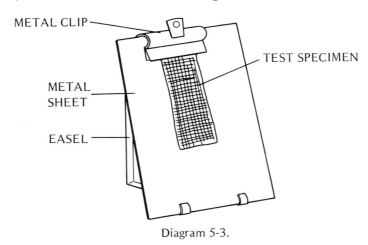

METAL CLIP

TEST SPECIMEN

METAL SHEET

EASEL

Diagram 5-3.

Apparatus for testing flammability of textiles. (N. B. This is not the apparatus used in testing to meet flammability standards for research.)

Procedure

1. Carry out testing in an area that is free from drafts where these activities will present no fire hazard. Perform the tests over a noncombustible surface. Work with a partner. One person will ignite the specimen and the other person will use the stopwatch in order to keep the records of time.

2. Fasten a test specimen to the metal clip, with the long dimension hanging downward. (See Diagram 5-3.)

3. Hold a lighted candle or Bunsen burner at the base of the fabric sample. The person with the stopwatch will time the period required to ignite the fabric. Record the time.

4. As soon as the fabric has ignited, remove the flame. Observe whether the fabric continues to burn or whether the flame goes out.

5. If the fabric sample continues to burn, record the time required for the sample to be consumed. If the flame goes out, record the time required for the flame to go out.

6. In fabrics that were not consumed by the flame, measure the char marks on the sample.

7. Record all of the data on Chart 5-4.

8. Repeat the experiment on all five specimens of the same fabric and average the data for the five burnings.

9. Repeat the experiment on the second test fabric. If additional fabrics are to be tested, repeat the experiment on each test fabric. Record all data on Chart 5-4.

10. If some specimens were not consumed in the experiment, they can be mounted at the back of the manual in the space provided for larger specimens.

CHART 5-4 FLAMMABILITY OF SELECTED TEXTILE FABRICS																								
Sample 1	Time of Ignition						Time of Burning before Being Consumed *OR* Self-Extinguishing												Length of Char					
	1	2	3	4	5	Average	1	2	3	4	5	Average	1	2	3	4	5	Average	1	2	3	4	5	Average
Fiber content: Special finishes:	1	2	3	4	5	Average	1	2	3	4	5	Average	1	2	3	4	5	Average	1	2	3	4	5	Average
Sample 2																								
Fiber content: Special finishes:	1	2	3	4	5	Average	1	2	3	4	5	Average	1	2	3	4	5	Average	1	2	3	4	5	Average
Sample 3																								
Fiber content: Special finishes:	1	2	3	4	5	Average	1	2	3	4	5	Average	1	2	3	4	5	Average	1	2	3	4	5	Average
Sample 4																								
Fiber content: Special finishes																								

Questions

. . . Which of the samples showed either flame retardancy or resistance to burning?

. . . Did any of these fabrics have a flame-retardant finish? Did those fabrics with flame-retardant finishes ignite?

Did they extinguish before being consumed?_____

. . . Which of the samples, if any, would you consider safe for children's sleepwear and why?

(5) Effect of Care Procedures on Flame-Retardant Finishes

Certain care procedures diminish the effectiveness of flame-retardant finishes. Students may wish to structure a research project that tests the effects of these care procedures on flame-retardant finishes. The procedures that may adversely affect flame-retardant finishes are

1. laundering with low phosphate detergents

2. laundering with chlorine bleach

3. laundering with fabric softeners

4. laundering with hard water

5. laundering with soap

UNIT 6

Care of Fabrics and Textiles and the Environment

PART 1: CARE LABELING

Reference: pp. 19, 20, 391 in *Understanding Textiles* or assigned readings in text or reference books.

1. Read the reference(s) outlining the provisions of the Care Labeling Regulations.

2. List the items that are not required to carry care labels.

PART 2: LAUNDRY ADDITIVES

Reference: Chapter 21, *Understanding Textiles* or assigned readings in text or reference books.

1. The instructor will divide the class into some or all of the following groups:

   Group 1: medium to high phosphate detergent, no bleach.
   Group 2: medium to high phosphate detergent, chlorine bleach.
   Group 3: medium to high phosphate detergent, perborate bleach
   Group 4: low phosphate detergent, no bleach
   Group 5: low phosphate detergent, chlorine bleach

Group 6: low phosphate detergent, perborate bleach

Group 7: soap, no bleach

Group 8: soap, chlorine bleach

Group 9: soap, perborate bleach

Group 10: any type of detergent, fabric softener added to the washer

Group 11: any type of detergent, fabric softener added in the dryer

****Materials and Apparatus

two, 5″ (13 cm) square test specimens of white cotton fabric for each student

two, 5″ (13 cm) square test specimens of white polyester fabric for each student

one 5″ (13 cm) square of cotton and one of polyester for control samples

normal detergent (medium to high phosphate)

low phosphate detergent

soap

chlorine bleach

perborate bleach

fabric softener: type added to rinse
type added to dryer

indelible pen

materials for staining fabric: greasy soil
earth soil

Procedure

1. Each student will stain one specimen of cotton and one specimen of polyester with greasy soil. Label each specimen with the name of the laundry product to be used, the type of fabric, and the type of soil. Use an indelible pen.

2. Each student will stain one specimen of cotton and one specimen of polyester with earth soil. Label each specimen with the name of the laundry product to be used, the type of fabric, and the type of soil.

3. Fabric specimens will be laundered in automatic washers at a laundromat.

4. Launder specimens following directions given on the laundry products being used. Run each set of specimens through the full wash-and-dry cycle. In order to make a full load for the washer it may be necessary to add one or two white bedsheets.

5. Display the laundered and dried specimens, so that students can compare the results of different types of laundering techniques. Include the control sample in the display so that laundered test specimens can be compared to the control.

6. Record the effectiveness of the laundering procedure used in removing the soil from the test specimen on Chart 6-1, then answer the questions that follow the chart.

CHART 6-1

Effectiveness of selected laundry procedures on two types of soil	GREASY SOILED SAMPLES			EARTH SOILED SAMPLES		
	medium-high phosphate detergent no bleach	medium-high phosphate detergent chlorine bleach	medium-high phosphate detergent perborate bleach	medium-high phosphate detergent no bleach	medium-high phosphate detergent chlorine bleach	medium-high phosphate detergent perborate bleach
Cotton						
Polyester						
	low phosphate detergent no bleach	low phosphate detergent chlorine bleach	low phosphate detergent perborate bleach	low phosphate detergent no bleach	low phosphate detergent chlorine bleach	low phosphate detergent perborate bleach
Cotton						
Polyester						
	soap no bleach	soap chlorine bleach	soap perborate bleach	soap no bleach	soap chlorine bleach	soap perborate bleach
Cotton						
Polyester						
	detergent, fabric softener in rinse cycle			detergent, fabric softener in rinse cycle		
Cotton						
Polyester						
	detergent, fabric softener in dryer			detergent, fabric softener in dryer		
Cotton						
Polyester						

Questions

. . .Which laundering technique seems to be most effective in removing greasy soil from the cotton samples? _____

_____

. . .Which laundering technique seems to be most effective in removing greasy soil from the polyester samples? _____

_____

. . .Was there any difference between the appearance of the cotton and polyester samples soiled with greasy soil? _____

_____

_____

. . .Which laundering technique seems to be most effective in removing earth soil from the cotton samples? _____

_____

. . .Which laundering technique seems to be most effective in removing earth soil from the polyester samples?_____

_____

. . .Was there any difference between the appearance of the cotton and the polyester samples soiled with earth soil? _____

_____

_____

. . .In general, which of the bleaches seemed most effective? _____

_____

_____

. . .In general, did the high-to-medium phosphate detergent, the low phosphate detergent, or the soap seem most effective without bleach? _____

_____

_____

_____

. . .Which of the fabric softeners seemed to produce a softer fabric? _____

_____

_____

PART 3: STAIN REMOVAL

References: Chapter 21, *Understanding Textiles, Removing Stains from Fabrics,* Washington D.C., U.S. Department of Agriculture, Home and Garden Bulletin, No. 63, 1973 and/or other assigned reference materials.

One aspect of caring for fabrics is the removal of soil and stains from the fabrics that may be acquired through use. To remove stains effectively, one must select a method that takes into account the type of fabrics on which the stain was made, as well as a type of remover that is appropriate to the stain.

Stain removal is easiest when the stain is fresh and becomes more difficult after the stain has been set. For this reason the samples to be used in the following experiment should be prepared at least three hours before the experiment is carried out.

*(1) Preparation of the Stained Samples

Materials and Apparatus

seven samples per student of white polyester/cotton blend fabric, each sample measuring about 4″ (10 cm) square, one to be used as a control sample

protective covering for the tabletop

indelible pen or pencil

ice cream sticks or tongue depressors

teaspoon

eyedropper

staining substances: coffee with cream

black coffee

mustard

mayonnaise

salad oil

ball-point pen

plastic wrap (optional)

file folders (optional)

Procedure

1. Place six samples of fabric on a protected surface. Retain one sample as a control sample.

2. Before applying the stain, write the name of the staining substance clearly in indelible ink at the top of the sample. Apply one stain to each fabric sample.

3. Stain the fabric samples as follows:
   a. Apply coffee with cream and black coffee by pouring a spoonful of fluid on each sample.
   b. Apply mustard and mayonnaise with an ice cream stick or tongue depressor.
   c. Apply salad oil with an eyedropper. Hold the eyedropper about three inches from the sample. Drop three or four drops on the sample.
   d. Make several lines with the ball-point pen on the sample.

4. Wait five minutes. If any stain residue remains on the surface of the fabric after five minutes, remove it with an ice cream stick or tongue depressor.

5. Store the samples until they are to be used. If the samples are to be kept for an extended period of time, they can be stored in file folders labeled with each student's name. Wrap the samples in plastic wrap to prevent the transfer of stains from one sample to another.

**(2) Stain Removal Laboratory

Materials

   prepared, stained samples
   variety of different commercial spot-and-stain-removal products
   detergent
   soap
   alcohol
   ammonia
   chlorine bleach
   supply of hot and cold water
   sponges and clean fabric for use with removers
   stain-removal charts, pamphlets, etc.

Procedure

1. The instructor will assign students to work in groups of two or three. Each student will have a full set of stained samples. This will provide at least two stained samples for each group.

2. From the reference materials provided by the instructor and from the text, each group should determine the best stain-removal procedure for each type of stain. Enter the description of this procedure on Chart 6-2.

3. Using the information from the reference material and following the recommended procedure, attempt to remove the stain from one sample. Compare the treated sample with the control sample. Enter a description of the results on Chart 6-2.

4. Evaluate the results. If this procedure was not successful in removing the stain, try a different procedure on the second stained sample. *Do not use more than one procedure on each stained sample, as one procedure may set the stain.* Compare the treated sample to the control. Enter a description of the results on Chart 6-2.

5. If the second procedure was not successful in removing the stain, determine from the reference material another technique that might be used to remove the stain. Enter this information on Chart 6-2 under "Other recommended treatments."

6. Mount the treated samples in the space provided on the chart.

CHART 6-2 STAIN REMOVAL

Staining Substance	Technique Used for Removal	Results	Mounted Samples
Coffee, black Specimen 1			
Specimen 2			
Other recommended treatments:			
Coffee with cream Specimen 1			
Specimen 2			
Other recommended treatments:			
Mustard Specimen 1			
Specimen 2			
Other recommended treatments:			
Mayonnaise Specimen 1			
Specimen 2			
Other recommended treatments:			
Salad oil Specimen 1			
Specimen 2			
Other recommended treatments:			
Ball-point pen Specimen 1			
Specimen 2			
Other recommended treatments:			

PART 4: TEXTILES AND THE ENVIRONMENT

Reference Chapter 22, *Understanding Textiles* or assigned readings in text or reference books.

Environmental problems relating to the production and use of textiles can be divided into four areas: dangers to the health of workers in the textile industry; pollution to air and water from textile manufacture; pollution of water from home laundering; and the energy required for the care of textile products.

(1) What is OSHA and what is its function in the textile industry?

(2) Contact the local environmental protection agency in your community and determine what rulings exist in your community concerning:
   a. Disposal of industrial wastes from textile manufacture and/or finishing.

   b. Use of soaps and detergents for home laundry.

(3) The home care of textile products requires the use of energy in the form of electricity and/or natural or bottled gas of which conservation is needed. In the space provided analyse the possible differences in energy requirements for home care of the following products: a white shirt made from 100 per cent cotton and a similar shirt made from 50 per cent cotton, 50 per cent polyester.

FACTORS TO CONSIDER:	COTTON	BLEND
Water temperature required		
Time required for laundering		
Time required for drying		
Pressing		

Which is likely to require less energy for care? Why? _____
_____
_____
_____
_____
_____
_____
_____
_____
_____
_____

UNIT 7

Textile Testing And Performance Evaluation

Reference Chapters 23 and 24 in *Understanding Textiles* or assigned chapters in other text or reference books.

PART 1: LEVELS OF TESTING

Many of the activities that have been described in this manual are simplified tests with limited control of testing conditions. In some cases no technical testing apparatus has been used, in some cases some elementary testing apparatus may have been employed, and in those laboratories where more sophisticated equipment is available students may have observed tests on this equipment or may have used the equipment themselves.

For research and industrial purposes only established tests, performed under specified conditions and using approved methods and equipment, are considered valid. The simplified type of testing described in most of this manual can provide only an approximation of textile behavior. Although much of this kind of evaluation is useful to the consumer or to the student to demonstrate certain properties, one should remember that there are many limitations to the kind of information it provides.

To demonstrate the differences between various levels of testing, three tests are described. All three are designed to test wrinkle recovery. The first is a simple test, performed without laboratory equipment. The second is an adaptation of a laboratory test that uses slightly more control and standardization of procedures. The third is a technical test established by the American Society for Testing Materials.

A. Test 1

*Materials and Apparatus

two samples of cotton fabric without special finishes, each 4″ (10 cm) square, one to be used as a control sample

two samples of polyester fabric, each 4″ (or 10 cm) square, one to be used as a control sample

watch for timing

Procedure

1. Crumple the test specimen of cotton fabric in the fist for one minute.

2. Release the specimen. Place it on a flat surface without smoothing or brushing out the specimen.

3. Compare it to the control sample of cotton fabric that has not been crumpled. Note the degree of wrinkling as (1) very wrinkled, (2) moderately wrinkled, or (3) slightly wrinkled.

4. Allow the specimen to recover for five minutes. At the end of five minutes determine whether the specimen has shown recovery from wrinkling or whether it remains wrinkled. Note the degree of wrinkling as (1) very wrinkled, (2) moderately wrinkled, or (3) slightly wrinkled.

5. Repeat the procedures in steps 1 and 4 for the polyester test specimen. Mount the tested specimens in the space provided.

cotton

degree of wrinkling is
immediately _____
after five minutes _____

polyester

degree of wrinkling is
immediately _____
after five minutes _____

Questions

. . . Is a standard of evaluation used? If so, what is it?

. . . What is the purpose of having a standard of evaluation?

. . . What are the limitations of a test of this kind?

. . . What are some of the conditions that are not controlled in this test?

B. Test 2

**Materials and Apparatus

 one sample of cotton and one sample of polyester fabric, each 5″ (13 cm) in the warp by 7″ (18 cm) filling

 two one pound (500 gram) weights

 watch for timing

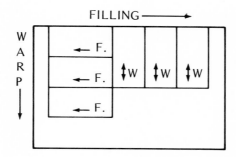

Diagram 7-1.
Preparation of Test Specimens for B., Test 2.

Procedure

1. From each fabric prepare six test specimens as follows: (See Diagram 7-1.)
 a. Cut three test specimens measuring 2 inches (5 cm) in the warp and 1 inch (2.5 cm) in the filling. Mark the specimen with a W.
 b. Cut three test specimens measuring 1 inch (2.5 cm) in the warp and 2 inches (5 cm) in the filling. Mark the samples with an F.
 c. Retain the rest of the specimen as a control sample against which to compare the tested specimens.

2. Allow the specimens to recover from handling for 10 minutes before testing.

3. Fold warp specimens in half across the two-inch dimension. (See diagram 7-2). Do not crease with the fingers.

4. Place each set of warp specimens under a one pound (or 500 gram) weight for five minutes.

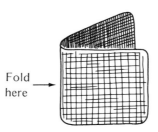

Diagram 7-2.
Folding of Test Specimens for B. Test 2.

5. Remove the weight from the warp test specimens. Do not touch the specimens. Observe the degree of creasing. Rate creasing and record rating on Chart 7-1 as (1) a very pronounced crease, (2) moderate crease, (3) little or no crease.

6. Allow warp specimens to recover for five minutes, then observe to determine whether creases remain or to what extent the creases have been removed. Rate creasing as (1) very pronounced crease, (2) moderate crease, or (3) little or no crease. Record rating.

7. Repeat steps 3 to 6 for the filling specimens.

8. Mount a sample of the fabric tested at the bottom of the page.

CHART 7-1 COMPARISON OF CREASING OF COTTON AND POLYESTER FABRICS				
	Cotton Specimens		Polyester Specimens	
	Warp Specimens	Filling Specimens	Warp Specimens	Filling Specimens
Degree of creasing: Immediately				
After five minutes				

Questions

In what ways is test no. 2 more controlled than test no. 1?

In what ways is test no. 2 still uncontrolled?

Can you suggest any ways in which test no. 2 could be given better control?

C. Test 3

*****[1] Read the instructions for ANSI/ASTM Test Method D 1295, printed in the *Annual Book of ASTM Standards* Part 33, "Wrinkle Recovery of Woven Textile Fabrics Using the Vertical Strip Apparatus." An illustration of the equipment used for this test is seen in Diagram 7-3. If equipment for this test is available and time permits, the test can be performed in the laboratory. If not, read through the test carefully and answer the following questions. If the test is to be performed, follow the instructions provided by the instructor, then answer the questions. Mount the tested samples in the space provided at the end of this section.

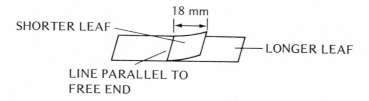

SPECIMEN HOLDER

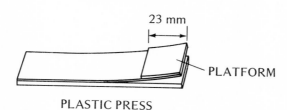

PLASTIC PRESS

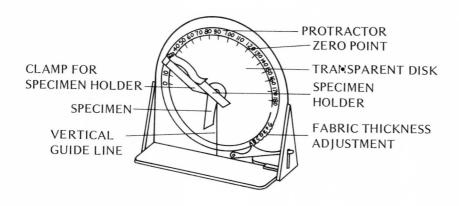

Diagram 7-3.

Wrinkle Recovery Tester

Reprinted by permission of the American Society
for Testing and Materials, D 1295, Part 32, *Annual
Book of ASTM Standards*.

[1] Test will require more than two hours. Preparation of specimens must be done in advance of the laboratory, as they must be conditioned at standard temperature and humidity for 24 hours before testing. Each test specimen (there are 12) requires time for mounting, five minutes of creasing and five minutes of recovery in the Wrinkle Recovery Tester. A three-hour laboratory should provide adequate time for all testing procedures.

1. Comparing the ASTM test method to tests 1 and 2, describe the ways in which the ASTM method provides more careful control of testing conditions than either of the other two tests.

2. What are some of the differences in the accuracy of the final rating or evaluation of the ASTM test and the other two tests?

3. What standard of evaluation is used in the ASTM test?

4. If you were a researcher or manufacturer, which of these three test results would you trust most and why?

5. What are some of the limitations of the ASTM test?

PART 2: EVALUATION OF TEXTILE PRODUCTS

When the consumer purchases a textile product, he or she takes into consideration the use to which that product will be put. Often the consumer's judgment about how a product will perform in a particular use will be a major factor in determining which one of several different products to purchase.

The person with some background and training in the field of textiles is equipped to be more analytical in the evaluation of a textile product than the average consumer. Also, this person may be acquainted with a variety of simple and complex methods of textile evaluation.

The following activity is suggested as a summary of the material in this manual. It requires careful consideration of the use to which a particular textile product will be put and a choice of simple or complex evaluations that are appropriate for this fabric. The instructor will recommend useful references for this project.

Procedure

1. Select a textile intended for a specific end use. *For example,* a textile might be selected that would be used in children's sleepwear, for arctic weather conditions, for table linens, active sports, evening wear, as a bedspread, or for bedsheets.

2. Determine and record at the time the fabric is acquired:
   a. fiber content (% of each generic fiber)[2]
   b. special finishes given to the fabric[2]
   c. care instructions

3. Analyze the types of examinations and evaluations that will be useful in determining whether this textile will be suitable for the projected end use. Keep in mind that it may be useful to have information about (1) fiber content, (2) yarn construction and type, (3) fabric construction, (4) dyeing and printing, (5) finishing, and (6) care procedures. Make a detailed list of the procedures that should be carried out on this fabric in order to evaluate it in relation to the proposed end use, and give the reasons why these evaluations were selected. In addition to the tests and procedures described in this manual, consult some of the sources listed in the bibliography for information about other tests and procedures.

4. The instructor may assign students to perform some of these tests in the laboratory, or the instructor may ask that some of these tests be performed outside of class. If so, perform the tests and record the results.

5. After completing any testing procedures, determine whether the fabric is suitable for the projected end use and state why. The following chart may help to organize this project, or, as an alternative, the instructor may wish to have the project organized as a term paper.

TEXTILE PRODUCT ANALYSIS CHART

Mount sample of fabric here.

Fiber content:

Special finishes:

Care instructions:

Projected end use:

(1) List the characteristics that this fabric should have in order to perform well in the projected end use.

---

[2]For this project do not select any fabric for which this information is not available.

(2) Identify the specific information or tests that would help in the evaluation of this fabric for the projected end use.
(Explain why each of these evaluations or tests would be useful)

. . . Information or testing related to fiber content:

. . . Information or testing related to yarn construction:

. . . Information or testing related to fabric construction:

. . . Information or testing related to dyeing or printing:

. . . Information or testing related to finishes:

. . . Information or testing related to care of fabric:

. . . Other useful information or testing:

(3) If tests were carried out, list the tests performed and describe the results.

(4) On the basis of these tests, is this fabric likely to perform satisfactorily in the projected end use? Why?

APPENDIX A
Bibliography

TEXTS, GENERAL REFERENCES, AND ENCYCLOPEDIAS

Alexander, P. R. *Textile Products: Selection, Use, and Care.* Boston: Houghton Mifflin Company, 1977

American Fabrics Encyclopedia of Textiles. Englewood Cliffs, N.J.: Prentice-Hall, Inc. 2nd Ed.

Collier, A. M. *Handbook of Textiles.* New York: Pergamon Press, 1970.

Dembeck, A. *A Guide to Man-made Textile Fibers and Texture Yarns of the World.* New York: United Piece Dye Works, 1964.

Denny, G. G. *Fabrics.* Philadelphia: J. B. Lippincott Co., 1962.

Dictionary of Textile Terms. Danville, Va.: Dan River Mills.

Harries, N., and T. Harries. *Textiles: Decision Making for the Consumer.* New York: McGraw-Hill, Inc., 1974.

Hollen, M., and J. Saddler. *Textiles.* New York: Macmillan Publishing Co., Inc., 1973.

Joseph, M. *Introductory Textile Science.* New York: Holt, Rinehart, and Winston, Inc., 1976.

Klapper, M. *Fabric Almanac.* New York: Fairchild Publications, Inc., 1971.

Labarthe, J. *Elements of Textiles.* New York: Macmillan Publishing Co., Inc., 1975.

Linton, G. E. *The Modern Textile and Apparel Dictionary.* Plainfield, N.J.: Textile Book Service, 1972.

Lyle, D. S. *Modern Textiles.* New York: John Wiley & Sons, Inc., 1976.

Moncrieff, R. W. *Man-made Fibres.* New York: John Wiley & Sons, Inc., 1975.

Potter, M. D., and B. P. Corbman. *Textiles, Fiber to Fabric.* New York: McGraw-Hill Book Company, 1975.

Pizzuto, J. *Fabric Science.* New York: Fairchild Publications, Inc., 1974.

Textile Fibers and Their Properties. New York: American Association of Textile Technologists and Burlington Industries, 1977.

Textile Handbook. Washington, D.C.: American Home Economics Association, 1974.

Tortora, P. *Understanding Textiles.* New York: Macmillan Publishing Co., 1978.

Wingate, I. B. *Dictionary of Textiles.* New York: Fairchild Publications, Inc., 1967.

Textile Fabrics and Their Selection. Englewood Cliffs, N. J.: Prentice-Hall, Inc., 1970.

Wingate, I. B., K. R. Gillespie, and B. G. Addison. *Know Your Merchandise.* New York: McGraw-Hill, Inc., 1975.

Woodhouse, J. M. *Science for Textile Designers.* London: Elek Science, 1976.

TEXTILES AS AN ART AND CRAFT

Albers, A. *On Weaving.* Middletown, Conn.: Wesleyan University, 1965.

Anderson, F. *Tie-Dyeing and Batik,* Secaucus, N. J.: Chartwell Books, Inc., 1977..

Castino, R. *Spinning and Dyeing the Natural Way.* New York: Van Nostrand-Reinhold Co., 1974.

Clark, L. J. *The Craftsman in Textiles.* New York: Praeger Publishers, Inc., 1968.

Dendel, E. W. *African Pacific Crafts.* New York: Taplinger Publishing Company, 1974.

Fannin, A. *Hand-spinning, Art and Technique.* New York: Van Nostrand-Reinhold Co., 1970.

Fuhrmann, B. *Bobbin Lace.* New York: Watson-Guptill, 1976.

Harvey, V. *Macrame.* New York: Van Nostrand-Reinhold Co., 1967.

Held, S. B. *Weaving.* New York: Holt, Rinehart, and Winston Inc., 1972.

Keller, I. *Batik: The Art and Craft.* Rutland, Vt.: Charles Tuttle Co., 1966.

Kluger, M. *The Joy of Spinning.* New York: Simon and Shuster, Inc., 1971.

Kramer, J. *Natural Dyes, Plants, and Processes.* New York: Charles Scribner's Sons, 1972.

Melen, L. *Knotting and Netting.* New York: Van Nostrand-Reinhold Co., 1972.

Nordfors, J. *Needle Lace and Needleweaving.* New York: Van Nostrand-Reinhold, 1972.

Regenstein, E. *The Art of Weaving.* New York: Van Nostrand-Reinhold Co., 1970.

Ward, M. *Art and Design in Textiles.* New York: Van Nostrand-Reinhold Co., 1973.

TEXTILE CARE

Detergents in Depth. Proceedings of Symposium sponsored by Soap and Detergent Association, March, 1974, Washington, D. C.

Moss, A. J. E. *Textiles and Fabrics: Their Care and Preservation.* New York: Chemical Publishing Company, 1961.

"Soaps and Detergents for Home Laundering." U. S. Department of Agriculture. Home and Garden Bulletin #139. Washington, D. C.: Revised 1973.

The Technology of Home Laundering. Textile Monograph #108. New York: American Association for Textile Technology, 1973.

TEXTILE CHEMISTRY

Carter, M. E. *Essential Fiber Chemistry.* New York: Marcel Dekker, Inc., 1971.

Mark, H. F., and N. G. Gaylord. *Encyclopedia of Polymer Science and Technology.* New York: Interscience Publishing, 1964–1971.

Peters, R. H. *Textile Chemistry. Vol. 1.* New York: American Elsevier Publishing Co., Inc., 1967.

Roff, W. J. *Handbook of Common Polymers.* Cleveland, Ohio: GRG Press, 1971.

TEXTILE TESTING, STANDARDS, AND LEGISLATION

Book of ASTM Standards. Philadelphia: American Society for Testing and Materials, published annually.

Booth, J. E. *Principles of Textile Testing.* New York: Chemical Publishing Company, 1969.

Earland, D., and D. Raven. *Experiments in Textile and Fibre Chemistry.* London: The Butterworth Group, 1971.

Grover, E., and D. S. Hamby. *Handbook of Textile Testing and Quality Control.* New York: Interscience Publishers, Inc., 1960.

Hall, M. *Chemical Testing of Textiles, A Laboratory Manual.* Revised edit. Alabama: Auburn University Printing Service, 1974.

Hall, M. *Practical Fiber Identification.* Alabama: Auburn University, Printing Service, 1976.

Rules and Regulations Under the Textile Fiber Products Identification Act, as Amended to Nov. 1, 1974. Washington, D. C.: Federal Trade Commission, 1974.

Technical Manual. Research Triangle Park, N.C.: American Association of Textile Chemists and Colorists, published annually.

Textile Flammability, A Handbook of Regulations, Standards, and Test Methods.

Weaver, J. W. *Analytical Methods for a Textile Laboratory.* Research Triangle Park, N. C.: American Association of Textile Chemists and Colorists, 1968.

Performance Requirements for Institutional Textiles. New York: American National Standards Institution, 1973.

Performance Requirements for Textile Fabrics. New York: American National Standards Institution, 1968.

APPENDIX B

Students' Appendix

I. USE OF THE MICROSCOPE

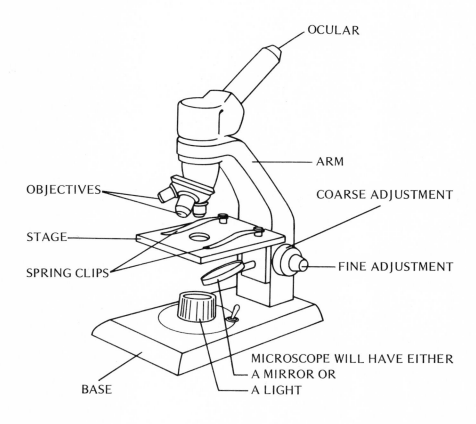

Figure B-1.
The microscope and its parts.

Although the examinations of fibers that are recommended in this manual will utilize slides prepared for viewing, some instructions on how to handle the microscope may be useful to those students who have not had previous experience with the instrument.

The following guidelines should be observed when the microscope is set up for use.

1. When lifting or moving the microscope, pick it up by the limb or arm.

2. Never work in direct sunlight.

3. Use a firm, steady table. The most comfortable seat for microscope work is a stool that can be adjusted to a comfortable height for viewing.

To view the prepared slide:

1. Turn the microscope to the objective you have been instructed to use. (The number of objectives and the magnification provided by each objective will differ from microscope to microscope.)

2. Raise the microscope as high as it will go.

3. Place the slide on the stage, with the fiber(s) centered over the opening for the light. Fasten the slide in place with the spring clips on the stage.

4. Lower the microscope until the objective is just a few centimeters above the slide. Do not allow the objective to touch the slide.

5. Look into the microscope. Turn on the illuminator or adjust the mirror to get the maximum amount of light into the microscope.

6. Start raising the microscope with the coarse adjustment knob. As soon as you get any view of the fiber, switch to the fine adjustment knob. With the fine adjustment knob, get the fiber clearly in view. Always focus the microscope by moving the objective up, never down. In moving the objective down you may break the slide and damage the lens.

For optimum viewing:

1. If you wear glasses, remove them for viewing.

2. Learn to look through the microscope with both eyes open. If you find this difficult, place your hand over one eye while observing with the other. Trying to keep one eye closed becomes very tiring after a while.

II. USE OF THE LINEN TESTER

The linen tester or pick glass, as it is also called, is equipped with a small magnifier mounted opposite a square opening at a distance providing needed focal depth. The most popular type is the folding linen tester. When placed on fabrics it provides a magnification of from 3.5 to 10. The base opening, usually one quarter inch square to one inch square, may have a calibrated edge to facilitate counting. See Figure B-2 for illustration of a folding linen tester.

To use the linen tester most effectively:

1. Lay the fabric to be examined on a flat surface.

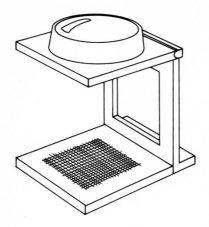

Figure B-2.
The linen tester.

2. Make sure that the area is adequately lighted. The source of light should be from the front or side as an overhead source of light will be blocked when one bends over the glass.

3. Place the square opening of the linen tester on the fabric. Align the bottom of the square along a filling yarn and the side of the square along a warp yarn.

4. View the fabric through the glass.

   The linen tester may also be used to examine individual yarns that have been un-raveled from a fabric sample. Place the yarn on a flat surface—a sheet of white paper makes a useful background. Place the linen tester over the sample and examine.

   A linen tester is often used in conjunction with a pick needle. A pick needle is a long, pointed, fine needle mounted in a handle or holder. The pick needle may be useful in separating yarns during counting or examination, and is used as a pointer. It can also be used to tease fibers apart during the examination of yarns.

Table B-1. Recommended Laundering Procedures			
Fiber	Time	Water Temperature	Agitation and Spin Speed
Wool	1–3 minutes	110°–120° F (43–49°C)	gentle
Cotton and linen	10–12 minutes	120°–140° F (49–60°C)	normal
Man-made and durable press	5–7 minutes	110°–120° F (43–49°C)	gentle

IV. TABLE B-2. COMMON METRIC EQUIVALENTS

U. S. Measurements	Metric Measurements
Length	Length
0.4 inch	1 centimeter
1.0 inch	2.5 centimeter
1.0 foot	0.3 meter
1.0 yard	0.0 meter
1.1 yards	1.0 meter
Volume	*Volume*
.06 cubic inch	1.0 cubic centimeter
1.0 cubic inch	16.4 cubic centimeters
1.0 teaspoon	5.0 milliliters
0.2 teaspoon	1.0 milliliter
1.0 cup	.24 liter
4.2 cups	1.0 liter
Temperature	*Temperature*
Fahrenheit	Celsius or Centigrade
0°	−17.9°
32° (freezing)	0° (freezing)
70°	21.1°
100°	43°
212° (boiling)	100° (boiling)

To convert F° to C°: subtract 32, multiply by 5, and divide by 9.

To convert C° to F°: multiply by 9, divide by 5, and add 32.

V. SAMPLE MOUNTING TECHNIQUES

Space has been provided throughout the manual for the mounting of swatches and test samples. These samples can be mounted as follows:

1. Mount all samples with the warp running vertically and the filling running horizontally.

2. Mount the sample with either tape or staples.

If staples are used, be sure to place the staples far enough from the edge of the sample to secure even those that may ravel.

If tape is used it may be possible to find tape with adhesive on both sides. Attach the tape to the back of the sample and then press the sample firmly in the mounting space. If double-faced tape is not available, either place a strip of regular tape across the top or one side of the sample, or make a hinge by folding the tape in half with the adhesive side out. Place half of the hinge against the page and half of the hinge against the back of the fabric.

3. Place the tape or staples along only one side of the swatch near the edge. If mounted in this way, it will be possible to examine both sides of the fabric after the sample has been mounted.

4. For some tests a small piece will be trimmed from the test specimen for mounting in the manual.

APPENDIX C

The Instructor's Guide to the Use of the Manual

I. SELECTION OF FABRIC SAMPLES

1. Use fabrics that will emphasize the subject matter that is stressed in the particular experiment. Avoid using any fabrics that will tend to obscure or confuse concepts.

2. Use fabrics of light colors or use white fabrics for greater visibility. Avoid the use of dark colors, especially black or navy blue.

3. Select fabrics without special finishes or surface effects that would obscure results of testing or observation. When testing for characteristics, such as absorbency, wrinkle resistance, and the like, launder samples before testing to remove waxes, oils, or other finishing materials that might interfere with experiments. Do not select fabrics with applied resin finishes unless this finish is part of the experiment.

4. When comparisons are being made between fibers or fabrics, be sure to use fabrics with comparable yarn construction, fabric construction, and count so that as many variables have been eliminated as possible.

5. When comparisons are being made between the effect of the yarn or a fabric construction, use fabrics made from the same fiber wherever possible to avoid confusion resulting from differing fiber characteristics.

6. Throughout the manual where fabric swatches are recommended for use for examination and identification, a size of 2 inches (5 cm) in the warp and 3 inches (8 cm) in the filling has been designated. Obviously instructors can use swatches of other dimensions, and the use of smaller swatches would permit the mounting of more samples where more are preferred. Additional pages are provided at the back of the manual for mounting additional or large test specimens. If the instructor wishes to supplement the number of samples recommended in any section, extra pages of samples can be inserted at appropriate places.

7. Wherever appropriate, select fabric samples that are popular currently or familiar to students.

II. EQUIPMENT

1. If the laboratory has adequate supplies available, each student could be issued the following basic set of laboratory supplies.

   linen tester
   pick needle
   pair of scissors
   tape or stapler for attaching samples to manual
   ruler, marked in both inches and centimeters

2. For those institutions with limited equipment, the following is a list of basic equipment needed for carrying out the simpler tests in this manual:

   microscope(s)
   linen testers
   pick needles
   stopwatch
   hot plate or Bunsen burner(s)
   balance(s)
   laboratory glassware: beakers, watch glasses, test tubes, graduated cylinders, stirring rods, eyedroppers
   laboratory thermometers
   small tongs
   screw-top jars

   Shortages of equipment can be overcome by the use of demonstrations, assigning students to work together in groups, or working out staggered schedules for use of items of equipment. Some items of equipment can be improvised or substitutions made.

III. ESSENTIAL REFERENCE MATERIALS FOR USE WITH THIS MANUAL

If possible, copies of these books should be available in the classroom or laboratory.

Book of ASTM Standards, parts 32 and 33. Philadelphia: American Society for Testing and Materials, published annually.

Technical Manual. Research Triangle Part, N. C.: American Association of Textile Chemists and Colorists, published annually.

Textile Handbook. Washington, D. C.: American Home Economics Association, 1974.

One or more of the following:

American Fabrics Encyclopedia of Textiles. Englewood Cliffs, N. J.: Prentice-Hall, Inc., 1972.

Dictionary of Textile Terms. New York: Dan River Company.

Klapper, M. *Textile Glossary.* New York: Fairchild Publications, Inc., 1973.

IV. GENERAL SUGGESTIONS FOR LABORATORY ORGANIZATION

1. Where samples of fibers or fabrics are in short supply or difficult to obtain, prepare one or more sets of large-size samples for demonstration and ask students to make careful note of characteristics they have observed.

2. For exercises such as differentiation of staple and filament yarns, identification of novelty yarns, identification of warp and filling knits, and other similar activities, prepare a master display of the samples. Use the format suggested in the manual for recording correct answers, and fill in the correct identifications. When students have completed the exercise, the master chart can be displayed and used by students or the instructor for checking the accuracy of the answers.

3. In a number of instances, activities recommended may require more time than the instructor has available in a laboratory or class period. Some ways of organizing the class to adjust to available time are

   a. Divide the class into groups, and ask each group to carry out one activity or part of an activity.

   b. Assign all or part of some activities to be done outside of class or laboratory time.

   c. Demonstrate the tests or experiments for the class.

   d. Avoid long periods of inactivity in the laboratory by staggering experiments so that some short procedures can be carried out while students are waiting for the completion of experiments that require samples to be laundered, dried, or otherwise treated.

IV. GUIDELINES TO SPECIFIC SECTIONS OF THE MANUAL

At the beginning of each activity in the manual that requires materials or apparatus is a list of (1) textile samples required for each student, (2) apparatus or equipment required for the tests or experiments, and (3) necessary laboratory supplies. From these the instructor can readily determine the total quantity of supplies and equipment needed and make the routine preparations necessary for each laboratory session.

A symbol is placed alongside tests and experiments to indicate the general time requirements of that activity. See page 3 for the listing.

The following pages consist of special suggestions for organizing the laboratory, obtaining supplies, and/or selecting sample materials that may prove helpful.

UNIT ONE: TEXTILE FIBERS AND THEIR PROPERTIES

Part 3: Physical Properties of Textile Fibers

A. Fiber Properties Relating to Appearance

2. Microscopic Appearance

Suggestions: 1. Directions for preparing slides of textile fibers are to be found in D. Hall, *Practical Fiber Identification.* Alabama: Auburn University Printing Service, 1976), pp. 2–8.

2. Photomicrographs of textile fibers are to be found in many introductory textiles texts.

3. Luster

Suggestion: One possible source of samples of bright and dull acetate filament fiber is the Technical Information Division of the American Enka Company, Enka, N. C. 28728.

4. Crimp

Suggestion: Obtain samples of crimped and uncrimped staple or filament from fiber manufacturing companies. Do not use samples of fiber unraveled from yarns, as the crimp of the yarn may be transferred to the fiber.

B. Fiber Properties Relating to Performance

1. Strength

Suggestion: If filament fibers cannot be obtained in sufficient quantities for the entire class, yarns can be unraveled from fabrics and each yarn untwisted to obtain a bundle of fibers. If the two yarns used are comparable in size, the fibers untwisted from one yarn may provide a bundle of fibers of convenient size for testing.

2. Specific Gravity

Suggestion: Specific gravity figures are to be found in *Understanding Textiles* and the *Textile Handbook* of the AHEA.

5. Resilience

Suggestions: 1. Use the same fabric for both wrinkle-recovery tests.

2. Be sure that the linen samples have not been given a wrinkle-recovery finish.

6. Absorbency

Suggestions: 1. If an oven is not available for drying samples of fabric, fabrics can be used without predrying; however, the instructor might discuss with students the reasons that predryed samples would yield more accurate results.

2. If a stopwatch is not available for timing the hoop test, use a digital wristwatch. Results will not be as accurate as with a stopwatch, but time will be more accurately kept than if an ordinary wristwatch is used.

9. Effect of heat, burning characteristics

(1) Effect of heat

Suggestions: 1. This test might make a suitable demonstration or could be performed by groups of students in view of the number of irons that would be required for the entire class.

2. If an iron that is calibrated in degrees rather than in fiber types is available, it should be used.

(2) Burning characteristics

Suggestion: Yarns for burning can be unraveled from fabric samples.

Part 4: Chemical Properties of Textile Fibers

Suggestions: 1. If the laboratory or classroom is not equipped for handling chemicals, the instructor may wish to set up a small laboratory area and demonstrate the experiments in this section.

2. If the laboratory has adequate facilities for carrying out the tests, but time limitations do not allow them to be done by each student, divide the tests among individuals or groups of students and have the results reported to the class.

Part 5: Generic Textile Fibers

Suggestion: A master fabric sample of 14 inches (35 cm) in the warp and 16 inches (40 cm) in the filling will be adequate to provide test specimens for one student to do all of the activities recommended in this section. If some tests are not performed, the size of the sample can be reduced accordingly.

UNIT TWO: YARNS

Part 1: Yarn Construction

(1) Hand Spinning

Suggestion: If instructors wish to demonstrate hand spinning but are not adept at spinning themselves, photographs and instructions are clearly presented in Ruth Castino, *Spinning and Dyeing the Natural Way* (New York: Van Nostrand-Reinhold Company, 1974), pp. 40–43 and 47–49.

(2) Distinguishing Filament from Staple Yarns and (3) Distinguishing Carded from Combed Yarns

Suggestion: Select only those fabrics in which both the warp and filling yarns are made from the same type of fiber in order to avoid confusion. For distinguishing carded and combed yarns be sure to include samples of both carded and combed yarns of both wool and cotton. Students may find it easier to distinguish combed and carded yarns if the wool samples are examined first.

Part 3: Types of Yarns

(2) Novelty Yarns

For this activity fabrics will be required that use the following types of yarns:
    bouclé
    ratiné
    flake or flock
    nub (knot, spot, or knop)
    slub
    thick-and-thin
    spiral or corkscrew
    snarl
    core-spun

(3) Textured Yarns

Suggestion: It is advisable to select textured fabrics that show clear contrast between texturing for stretch and texturing for bulk. If yard goods cannot be obtained, consider using samples cut from garments such as hosiery or knitwear. Knitting yarns can also be used.

Part 4: Yarn Analysis

Suggestion: Because brocade fabrics often contain a variety of different yarn types within one fabric, they may be good choices for yarn analysis exercises. Fabrics for home decoration also offer yarn variety.

UNIT THREE: FABRIC CONSTRUCTION

Part 2: Woven Fabrics

A. Basic Weaves The Plain Weave

(3) Examination and Identification of Standard Fabrics in the Plain Weave
Some of the types of standard fabrics that might be used for swatching are

chambray	batiste	nainsook
gingham	voile	longcloth
crinoline	chiffon	muslin
cheesecloth	challis	crash
organdy	percale	butcher linen
organza	gauze	homespun

B. Basic Weaves Plain Weave Variations

(1) Examination and Identification of Standard Fabrics in the Basket Weave
Some of the types of standard fabrics that might be used for swatching are

monk's cloth

novelty fabrics using the basket weave

oxford cloth

hopsacking

(2) Rib and Cord Variations of the Plain Weave

Some of the types of standard fabrics that might be used for swatching are

crosswise ribs:

small ribs: broadcloth
poplin
taffeta

larger ribs: faille
grosgrain
reps

largest ribs: bengaline
ottoman
large reps

irregular ribs: shantung

lengthwise ribs or cords:

bedford cord
dimity

C. Basic Weaves The Twill Weave

(3) Examination and identification of standard fabrics in the twill weave.

Some of the types of standard fabrics that might be used for swatching are

even-sided twills: serge
surah
some flannels

warp-faced twills: denim
jean
drill
gabardine

others: herringbone
        star check
        houndstooth check

D. Basic Weaves The Satin Weave

(3) Examination and identification of standard fabrics in the satin and sateen weaves.

Some of the types of standard fabrics that might be used for swatching are

satin fabrics: sateen:

crepe-backed satins   cotton sateen
antique satin
double-faced satin
peau de soie
slipper satin

E. Fancy Weaves

Some of the types of standard fabrics that might be used for swatching are

(1) Jacquard Weave   (2) Dobby Weave
    brocade   bird's eye or diaper cloth
    damask   figured madras
    brocatelle   pique, especially waffle or
                                            honeycomb
                                        white-on-white figured shirtings

F. Other Weaves

(1) Leno Weave   (2) Woven Pile Fabrics
    grenadine   corduroy
    marquisette   velveteen
                                        velvet
                                        terry cloth

(3) Surface Weaves

Suggestion: Samples of these fabrics may be difficult to locate; therefore, space has been left for those fabrics that instructor can find and wishes to use. Where yardage is not adequate for all students to have a sample, instructors may prefer to prepare samples for examination, ask students to note their characteristics, and record the definitions without mounting any of the samples in their manuals.

(5) Multicomponent Fabrics—Interwoven Fabrics

Suggested fabric types:

sample 1: 3 sets of yarns. double-faced satins
                             some blanket fabrics
sample 2: 4 sets of yarns. matelasse
sample 3: 5 sets of yarns. coating fabrics, sometimes made with one
                             side of the fabric in one color, the other
                             side in a different color.

(8) Triaxial Fabrics

Samples of triaxial fabrics are not readily available. In the event that these fabrics do come into wider use and availability, space is left for mounting a sample.

Part 3: Knitted Fabrics

(1) Identification of wales and courses in knit fabric and (2) gauge count

Suggestion: Select fabrics for examination that have fairly large gauge to increase visibility of stitches.

A. Filling or Weft Knits and *B. Warp Knits*

Suggestion: Select fabrics for swatching that have marked contrasts in fiber content, yarn construction, textures, gauge, and hand in order to demonstrate the variety of fabrics that can be made by using the same type of knit construction with different components.

C. Distinguishing Warp and Filling Knits

Suggestion: Prepare a set of samples following the instructions in the manual so that students have a set of samples against which to check their own work.

D. Performance of Knit Fabrics

(1) Dimensional Stability

Suggestions: 1. Select fabrics for this experiment carefully. In order to obtain maximum contrasts in behavior, use some warp and some filling knits, some single and some double knits, and different fibers, such as acrylics, wool, cotton, polyester, or blends.

2. This project would lend itself to assignment as a research project for one or more students.

Part 4: Other Fabric Constructions

A. Nets, Lace, Macrame, and Crochet

Suggestion: Macrame and crochet, being hand processes, may not be available for swatching. If there are students in the class who are skilled in these methods of construction, they could demonstrate the technique for other students.

B. Stitch-through Fabric Construction

Suggestion: If samples of these fabrics are difficult to obtain, sources might be suggested by the Bahlo Textile Corporation, 850 Third Avenue, New York, N. Y. 10022.

C. Fabric Webs

Suggestion: The following companies produce trademarked fiber webs and may be able to suggest sources of samples of these fabrics.

Remay, Typar, Tyvek made by E. I. Du Pont de Nemours & Co.
Cerex made by Monsanto
Nexus made by Du Pont and Burlington Industries

UNIT FOUR: DYEING AND PRINTING

Part 1: Dyeing

(1) Identifying fiber, yarn, and piece-dyed fabrics.

Suggestion: Use only samples made from 100 per cent of the same generic fiber.

(2) Differences in Fiber Absorbency

Suggestion: 1. Dyes intended for home use such as Rit, Tintex, or craft dyes can be used. In order to save laboratory time, dye solutions can be prepared in sufficient quantity for the entire class before the laboratory period begins. 2. Select a fabric for this experiment that is made of a blend of two fibers with markedly different absorbency.

(3) Cross-dyeing and Union Dyeing

T. I. S. Identification Stain #1 is available from Testfabrics Inc., P. O. Box 118, 200 Blacksford Ave., Middlesex, N. J. 08846.

Part 2: Colorfastness

Suggestions: 1. Colorfastness tests can be performed by groups of students with each group carrying out a different test. Results can be reported to the rest of the class.

2. Multifiber Fabric can be obtained from Testafabrics Inc., P. O. Box 118, 200 Blacksford Ave., Middlesex, N. J. 08846.

Part 3: Printing

Swatches of the following printed fabrics are recommended for use in this section:
>roller print, multiple colors used
>warp print
>discharge print
>flock print
>heat transfer print
>duplex print

UNIT FIVE: FINISHES

Part 1: Classification of Finishes

Suggestion: Prepare starched samples following directions on the household starch container. Do not use spray starches that may be made to last through several launderings.

Part 2: Finishes Affecting Appearance

Swatches of the following fabrics are recommended for this section:
>polished cotton or chintz
>ciré
>embossed design
>moiré
>napped fabric: cotton flannel or napped wool
>flocked fabric: suedelike finishes on woven backing
>are often produced by flocking

>burnt-out design
>acid print
>plissé
>seersucker

Part 3: Finishes Affecting Performance

A. Test 1: *Evaluation of Dimensional Change of Laundered Woven Fabrics*

Suggestions: 1. This experiment can be done outside of class by students if the laboratory does not have laundering equipment. Students can add the samples to their own or the family laundry.

2. Because of the quantity of fabric required for this test if each student launders two samples, instructors may wish to select only three or more samples for laundering. Data can be given to the entire class, and all students would be asked to calculate the shrinkage.

B. Test 2: *Absorbency*

Suggestions: 1. If a stopwatch is not available, use a digital watch. The results, however, will be less exact with a digital watch.

2. Use fabrics as similar in fiber content as possible to avoid obtaining results that are the result of fiber content rather than finish. Also, select fabrics with comparable weaves and thread counts.

3. Comparable fabrics made with and without durable press finishes would provide an interesting contrast as would fabrics with and without the following finishes:

  soil resistant

  soil releasing

  water repellent

  antistatic

4. If comparable fabrics with and without soil-resistant finishes cannot be obtained, test samples can be prepared by spraying one set of specimens with Scotchgard.

5. Test unfinished samples only after they have been laundered to remove routine finishing materials such as waxes, starches, and the like.

C. Test 3: *Water Repellency*

Suggestion: 1. For laboratories without the testing apparatus, this apparatus can be constructed following directions in the AATCC Test Method 22-1974.

2. Standard Spray Test Rating Chart available from AATCC, P. O. Box 12215, Research Triangle Park, N. C., 27709.

D. Test 4 Fire-Retardant Finishes

Suggestions: 1. The potential fire hazards from burning fabrics in the laboratory may lead the instructor to demonstrate this test rather than to have students carry out the testing. An assistant is required, and the test area must be free from drafts. Test over a fireproof surface and protect the surface against damage from flaming melt that may drop onto the tabletop.

2. Recommended fabrics for testing:
  - cotton flannel taken from purchased sleepwear for children
  - cotton flannel yard goods not treated for flame retardancy
  - fabrics inherently flame retardant such as modacrylic or Cordelan
  - polyesters, both those treated for flame retardancy and those that have not been so treated.

UNIT SIX: CARE OF FABRICS AND TEXTILES AND THE ENVIRONMENT

Part 2: Laundry Additives

Suggestion: Samples of fabric can be prepared in class. If assigning the entire class to go to a laundromat is impractical, students can be asked to launder samples outside of class using the assigned technique. Laundered samples can be displayed in class so that students can compare the results.

2. In order to have a full load of wash for laundering, one or two old white sheets can be added to the washer.

Part 3: Stain Removal

Suggestion: Since stains must be prepared well in advance of this experiment, students could prepare them in one class or laboratory session for use at the next.

Part 4: Textiles and the Environment

Suggestion: Instructors may prefer to give students little or no guidance on how to obtain the names and locations of local environmental protection agencies in order to give students experience in tracking down this type of information.

UNIT SEVEN: TEXTILE TESTING AND PERFORMANCE EVALUATION

Part 1: Levels of Testing

C. Test 3

Note: This test requires that no specimens be cut nearer to the selvage than 1/10th the width of the fabric.

Suggestion: If only one tester is available, this test might be demonstrated by the instructor or students, or students may be assigned the use of the equipment on a rotating basis while other laboratory activity is in progress.

Part 2: Evaluation of Textile Products

Suggestions: 1. Fabrics used in this section can be provided by the instructor or obtained by students. In either case, samples of adequate size for testing can be obtained by purchasing yard goods or other small items such as towels, pillowcases, napkins, place mats, or children's apparel. Retail stores may have samples of discontinued fabrics for carpets, draperies, or bedspreads that they would be willing to give to students.

2. The project may be introduced early in the term so that students can perform tests on fabrics as each relevant area is covered in assigned readings, class lectures, and/or laboratory periods.

3. If the instructor prefers, the project can be carried out as a written exercise without the testing portion. Instead students can identify the appropriate tests that would be used for the evaluation of the fabric. Simple activities such as thread count could be done.

MOUNT EXTRA SAMPLES HERE